STUDENT LEADERSHIP UNIVERSITY
STUDY GUIDE SERIES

IDENTITY THEFT

JAY STRACK

D1308284

NELSON IMPACT
A Division of Thomas Nelson Publishers
Since 1798

www.thomasnelson.com

Published by Nelson Impact, a Division of Thomas Nelson, Inc., P.O. Box 141000, Nashville, TN 37214.

All Scripture quotations are taken from *The New King James Version®*. Copyright © 1982 by Thomas Nelson, Inc. Used by permission. All rights reserved.

ISBN 1-4185-0594-3

Printed in the United States of America

06 07 08 RRD 9 8 7 6 5 4 3 2

Page design by Crosslin Creative
2743 Douglas Lane, Thompsons Station, Tennessee 37179

CONTENTS

INTRODUCTION

Welcome to the no-holds-barred, in-your-face curriculum that dares to give you straight talk about some of the most controversial and forbidden topics that you are facing today. Did you know that you are being threatened even as you're reading this? The truth is that there are enemies waiting at your door. And not just at the door of your home or school or church—this is personal.

Governments throughout the world have launched fraud alerts against the ever-growing crime of identity theft. Every day, thieves all over the globe are taking bits and pieces of personal information and stealing the identities of others. Did you know you were at risk? Maybe your bank account is ok, but what about the thieves that are targeting your soul? These thieves are different—they want to rob you of your future, your reputation, and your spiritual identity.

Who are these thieves? They are many, and you're sure to recognize a few of them—sexual experimentation, alcohol, drugs, culture control, self-sabotage, loss of faith. Long, long ago, Jesus knew about these thieves and warned us:

> *The thief does not come except to steal,*
> *and to kill, and to destroy.*
> *I have come that they may have life,*
> *and that they may have it more abundantly.*

(John 10:10 NKJV)

Are you ready to defend yourselves from these thieves? Student Leadership University has gone undercover to expose this gang of thieves and their *modus operandi*. This study will give you the tools to fight and defend your identity.

KEY

STUDENT LEADERSHIP UNIVERSITY CURRICULUM

Throughout this study guide, you will see several icons or headings that represent an idea, a statement, or a question that we want you to consider as you experience Scripture in this study guide series. Refer to the descriptions below to help you remember what the icons and headings mean.

transfuse (trans FYOOZ)ː to cause to pass from one to another; transmit

The goal of the lesson for the week.

Experience Scripture: Learning to really experience Scripture is the key element to "getting" who God is and all that He has in store for you.

infuse (in FYOOZ)ː to cause to be permeated with something (as a principle or quality) that alters usually for the better

Through journaling, group discussion, and personal study, experience Scripture as it permeates your heart and alters your life.

Future Tense Living: Your choices today will determine your future. Learn how to live with dynamic purpose and influence.

Attitude Reloaded: Rethink your attitude! Learn to replace self-centered, negative, or limited thoughts with positive, courageous, compassionate thoughts that are based on God's unlimited ability and power.

 In His Steps: Every attitude and action of your life should begin with the questions, How would Jesus respond to this person and situation before me? What would He choose to do?

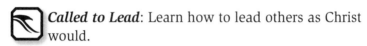

diffuse (di FYOOZ) : to pour out and permit or cause to spread freely; to extend, scatter

Once God's Word is infused into your heart, it will pour forth to others without restraint. In this section, explore what that looks like in your daily life.

Called to Lead: Learn how to lead others as Christ would.

Called to Stand: Know what you believe and learn how to defend it with clarity and strength.

Called to Share: Sharing truth and serving others are results of a transformed life. How can you share with others the awesome things you're learning?

One Thing: Consider ONE THING you can do this week to make a difference in your life and/or the life of another.

Power up for the week with this focused truth.

ID THIEVES AT THE DOOR

THEY COME TO DESTROY

KEY SCRIPTURE

The thief does not come except to steal, and to kill, and to destroy. I have come that they may have life, and that they may have it more abundantly.

—**John 10:10**

COULD THIS BE YOU?

The Thief: When Frank Abagnale was sixteen, his parents divorced, and the judge gave him the choice to live either with his mother or his father. Frank says, "I didn't really want to make that choice, and I was kind of stubborn. I just walked out of the courtroom, and basically ran away from home. No one wanted to hire a 16-year-old, but I was 6 feet tall, I had grey hair, and my friends always said I looked more like I was 28 years old. So I changed my date of birth on my driver's license so that it showed me as being 26 years old. I just took on that identity of being ten years older than I was, and that led to all the different jobs I took on, and all the different things I did."[1] In a five-year spree of forgery and fraud, as portrayed in the 2002 movie *Catch Me If You Can*, Abagnale impersonated his way around the United States, assuming identities as he went. He cashed $2.5 million in fraudulent checks in every state and in twenty-six foreign countries during a five-year period. Between the ages of sixteen and twenty-one, he successfully posed as an airline pilot, an attorney, a college professor, and a pediatrician before being apprehended by the French police.[2]

The Victim: "Imagine that an individual you have never met nor wronged has taken your identity with the intention of abusing your good name and unblemished credit profile."[3] Michelle Brown didn't have to imagine this. As she stated in her testimony before the U.S. Senate Committee, she was an ongoing victim of identity theft. Another woman used Michelle's name and good credit to rack up debt in excess of fifty thousand dollars. Because the woman impersonating Michelle was also involved in drug trafficking, not only was Michelle's credit ruined, but a warrant was issued in her name. The imposter was booked in a Chicago federal prison under the name Michelle Brown, and even after being released from prison, the other woman was still able to use Michelle's information for an additional six months.

Disciple: one who accepts and assists in spreading the doctrines of another.
—Merriam-Webster Dictionary

WHY KNOW IT?

✦ Identity thieves rob more than 500,000 Americans every year.[4]

✦ College students tend to see themselves as less spiritual by the end of their junior year than when they first entered college.[5]

✦ Sociologists say about twenty new religions pop up each year in the United States.[6]

✦ Nearly one-third of Americans will change religions at least once in their lifetime.[7]

✦ 40 percent of Christians contend that "the Bible, the Koran, and the Book of Mormon are all different expressions of the same spiritual truths." [8]

transfuse (trans FYOOZ) : to cause to pass from one to another; transmit

There is another form of identity theft taking place among Christian students. People in record numbers are simply walking away from what they once believed in and are assuming the spiritual identity of the crowd or the popular culture around them.

The thief does not come except to steal, and to kill, and to destroy. I have come that they may have life, and that they may have it more abundantly. —**John 10:10**

Make no mistake about it—there are forces at work in our culture that want to rob you of your identity as a Christian. And there are two methods of operation these forces employ: to *steal your identity* and/or to *entrap you* so you willingly give it up. Instead of a pure, peaceful identity as a child of God, they want you to be a confused, weak-willed person, one who is spiritually impotent and emotionally unhealthy.

When Jesus began His ministry, the crowds around Him were huge. Thousands followed Him looking for the Messiah, for healing, for deliverance. In John 6, we read one of the most significant miracles of Jesus, given in great detail. It is so significant that it is one of the few miracles recorded in all four of the Gospels: the feeding of the five thousand men. The word translated "men" is gender specific, because in that day only the men were numbered. Commentators tell us that women and children most likely made up to another fifteen thousand in attendance.

John 6 reveals the kind of messiah that the people wanted. They wanted a superhero kind of guy who could do wonders and fill their bellies at the same time. In fact, the chapter begins by saying, "A great multitude followed Him because they saw His signs that He had performed on those who were diseased" (v. 2). The story continues with more crowds beginning to follow Jesus—a generation seeking to fill their bellies and be entertained.

Do a heart check: Do you most often go to God in prayer only because you need something or need an answer?

Make a choice to go to Him in prayer daily to thank and praise Him just for Who He is—the God of love, forgiveness, and faithfulness (just to name a few!).

> *Jesus answered them and said, "Most assuredly,*
> *I say to you, you seek Me, not because you saw*
> *the signs, but because you ate of the loaves and*
> *were filled."*
> **(John 6:26)**

You might say they were looking for dinner and a movie. Jesus knew this, and He gave them more than they asked for. In fact, He demonstrated His ability to do so "abundantly," as He promised in John 10:10.

> *"Do not labor for the food which perishes, but*
> *for the food which endures to everlasting life,*
> *which the Son of Man will give you, because*
> *God the Father has set His seal on Him." Then*
> *they said to Him, "What shall we do, that we*
> *may work the works of God?" Jesus answered*
> *and said to them, "This is the work of God, that*
> *you believe in Him whom He sent."*
> **(John 6:27–29)**

When it became clear that the crowds were growing and His popularity was increasing, Jesus knew it was time for a reality check. He ended the superhero talk as He began to speak of being the Messiah, the Savior, who came to save the people from the pollution, pain, and penalty of their sin. They spoke of popularity and power—but He came to deliver them from helplessness, despair, loneliness, failure, and fear of death.

infuse (in FYOOZ)˙, to cause to be permeated with something (as a principle or quality) that alters usually for the better

"Jesus said to them, 'I am the bread of life. He who comes to Me shall never hunger, and he who believes in Me shall never thirst'" (John 6:35). In this verse, which is the climax of John 6, we learn two life-changing thoughts that Jesus gave the crowd and that He wants us to get:

1. Don't focus on the temporary (such as food and signs). Focus on eternal life.

2. Personal faith in Christ is power in the present and hope in the future.

Jesus's emphasis here is on the spiritual and on a single act of faith. The religion of Judaism emphasized many works, just like some religions do today. But Jesus reduces it all to one necessary act of personal faith—the one act essential to salvation, and the only one that can change the heart. In the midst of all the crowds, Jesus was confronting their motives.

Don't settle for "discount discipleship," a faith that only works in the easy times. Or for "theme-park Christianity," a faith focused on entertainment, events, and crowds instead of a personal journey of faith. Salvation is not about going on a different, more thrilling ride whenever boredom sets in.

Jesus confronted the selfishness of the crowd. Then He took it a step further: "He who eats My flesh and drinks My blood abides in Me, and I in him" (John 6:56).

The people didn't like this kind of talk. Feeding the crowds was exciting and watching the lame being healed was mind blowing, but what was this talk of eating flesh and drinking blood? Even His disciples said, "This is a hard saying" (v. 60).

Has something similar ever happened to you? You love the youth events with great music and entertainment, and you are eager to talk about those things. But when it comes to talking about your personal faith in the Savior, do you back off the discussion?

Why do you think this happens?

What happens next in this scene from Jesus's life is the most tragic verse in the entire Bible: "From that time many of His disciples went back and walked with Him no more" (v. 66). Not only did the crowd give up on His "hard saying," but some of Jesus's disciples left as well.

Who were the people who turned and left Jesus? These were not His random friends or casual acquaintances; they were His *disciples*. They changed their identity from pupils and devoted followers to quitters who looked for an easy message. The song changed, and they didn't like it.

Have you ever been a disciple who "went back and walked with Him no more"? If so, when? What was the setting you were in?

_____

_____

_____

Who was there at the time?

_____

_____

Were you angry, depressed, embarrassed? List what you were feeling at the time.

_____

_____

_____

Describe why you think it happened. What became "too hard"?

_____

_____

_____

> I have one life and one chance to make it count for something. . . . My faith demands that I do whatever I can, wherever I am, whenever I can, for as long as I can, with whatever I have to try to make a difference.
> —President Jimmy Carter

diffuse (di FYOOZ) : to pour out and permit or cause to spread freely; to extend, scatter

Imagine the sadness in Jesus's eyes when He asked the twelve disciples, "Do you also want to go away?" (John 6:67). Peter answered with an insightful question: "Lord, to whom shall we go? You have the words of eternal life" (v. 68).

This was just the opportunity Jesus needed to help each of the twelve understand their own hearts. As the crowd ran away, some of Jesus's disciples "went back and walked with Him no more" (v. 66). Now what would these twelve leaders—passionate followers of Christ—do?

Think of the three kinds of people in this story: the crowd, the disciples who went back, and the twelve who stayed strong. Which category do you fall into?

Which one would you like to be in?

What steps can you take to be a leader in your youth group who follows even the "hard sayings" when it comes to the truth of God's Word?

When you know the Word of God, then you will not be led away by every new religion or the current of the culture. With 58 percent of students dropping out of church once they leave home, the logical question is, to whom will you go?[9] Will you also change your identity, or just give up?

Here are some of the thieves waiting at your door to rob you of joy, peace, and the abundant life that Christ died to give you:

+ Friends (or "the crowd")

+ Alcohol and other drugs

+ The past

+ Sexual experiences and experiments

+ Self-sabotage

+ Changing who you are to fit in

+ Self-destruction from excuses

If you've already lost your true, pure identity as a Christian, know that Christ is ready to get you back on track. If you haven't ventured from the path of Christ, you need to stay strong and focused.

People are wondering if there is anything such as absolute truth. You can tell them, but more importantly, you can show them by demonstrating a genuine compassion. It is your responsibility to live in such a way that your identity in Christ will be clear to others and significant to you.

What is ONE THING you can do this week to share a spiritual truth with someone?

_____

_____

_____

Can you think of a particular person you can share this truth with?

_____

_____

_____

We all need a little help to keep the identity of who we are in Christ. The lessons that follow for the next seven weeks will provide you with understanding, strength, and passion for an incredible journey. Are you ready?

_____

_____

_____

FUSE BOX

There are identity thieves at the door of every heart. They wait for the chance to rob the genuine joy, peace, and confidence of Christ and replace it with the counterfeit and temporary offerings of the culture. Only you decide whether to open the door or not.

The first time that the followers of Christ were called Christians was in Acts 11:26. They were so designated because of what they believed, how they behaved, and to whom they belonged. Their identity was sure and strong.

PRIVATE WORLD DEVOTIONS

MONDAY: See it. Read the surrounding passages or chapter for the Key Scripture so that you can get an understanding of the background and context. This helps you to really *see* the verse.

TUESDAY: Hear it. Read the daily Key Scripture and/or surrounding passage out loud, putting your name in, if applicable. For example, <u>John</u> *can do all things through Christ. Thieves have come to destroy* <u>John</u>, *but Jesus has come that* <u>John</u> *might have eternal life.*

WEDNESDAY: Write it. Write the verse and then what it says about:

✦ *Others:* Respond, serve, and love as Jesus would.

✦ *Me:* Specific attitudes, choices, or habits.

✦ *God:* His love, mercy, holiness, peace, joy, etc.

PRIVATE WORLD JOURNAL

I am grateful for—I praise you for—I am feeling—I am thinking—I need help with

PRIVATE WORLD DEVOTIONS *(Continued)*

THURSDAY: Memorize it. Take the verse with you—write it on a card or put it in your phone, iPod, or PDA. Go over it throughout the day so that it begins to *live* in your heart and mind.

FRIDAY: Pray it. Personalize the verse as you pray for yourself or for others or in praise to God. To pray is literally "to think about." Try thinking out loud or writing in your **PRIVATE WORLD JOURNAL.**

SATURDAY: Share it. Ask the Lord to bring someone to mind or in your path today who needs good news. Don't be shy—just let it out! Whether you IM, write, text, tell, or send it, the joy of God's Word will flow from your heart into theirs.

PRAYER REQUESTS

Date	Name	Need	Answer

PRIVATE WORLD JOURNAL

I am grateful for—I praise you for—I am feeling—I am thinking—I need help with

NOTES

CHAPTER 2

LOST IN THE CROWD

THE FORCE OF CULTURE CONTROL

KEY SCRIPTURE

A man who has friends must himself be friendly, but there is a friend who sticks closer than a brother.

—Proverbs 18:24

COULD THIS BE YOU?

When Jeremy's brothers left for college, he found himself alone for the first time and needing a new best friend. He had never been part of the crowd, and now in his junior year, he found himself suddenly defined as the new guy on the block.

Jeremy quickly found out that the church kids already had their cliques, and getting in with them wasn't easy. They were friendly at church, but he never heard from any of them during the week. There was one group at school, though, who invited him again and again to their parties. They called and IM'd him often, telling long stories about girls and guys hooking up, drinking parties, and where to score the best drugs.

It finally hit Jeremy one day: *There must be someone else like me who is looking for friends who aren't holier than thou or going the drug and sex route.* He prayed, "Lord, show me that person I could befriend." That weekend at a church event, Jeremy noticed Tim across the room. Tim had punked-out hair and body piercings, and he stuck out in this church crowd. No one said a word to him.

Jeremy made his way across the room to Tim. At the end of the night, these two very different guys found out they had a lot in common, including sports, science fiction novels, and an interest in Scripture. Tim confided that he was also tempted to choose the wrong crowd because they were the only ones who befriended him.

Jeremy and Tim became accountability partners, and their friendship continued to grow throughout high school and college.

WHY KNOW IT?

✦ Loneliness is a major factor in teen suicide. Suicide is the third leading cause of death for 15- to 24-year-olds and the fourth for 10- to 14-year-olds,[1] with no signs of letting up.[2]

✦ Gossip and paparazzi photos are big business, and the demand is stronger than ever.[3] Each week the *National Enquirer*'s circulation tops 2.7 million,[4] and the *Globe*'s circulation reaches 1 million.[5]

transfuse (trans FYOOZ)*;* to cause to pass from one to another; transmit

Before buying a house or moving into a new neighborhood, you might drive the streets to see what kind of activity takes place in the neighborhood. Maybe you meet some of the neighbors, ask about the people who live in the area, and possibly even do a criminal check for sex offenders in the area. If this is going to be where you live, you want to know who else is living nearby, right? It should be the same when choosing friends to hang out with. Who's in the crowd? What do they believe, care about, and do in their free time? Is this a "neighborhood" you want to be a part of?

The friends you choose to walk alongside will become your emotional neighborhood and can make the difference in how you react to the pressure of grades, cliques, and the labels of "winner" or "loser." Often, the opinion of a friend will influence your choices and emotions, even to the point of replacing the opinion or rules of a parent. Choosing the right friends is a critical task.

Throughout the Bible, we see the power of strong, healthy friendships demonstrated in the stories of Ruth and Naomi, David and Jonathan, and Paul and Timothy. We are also given examples of the results of unhealthy friendships in the lives of Job and Samson.

So, according to the Bible, what does it take to have a healthy friendship? The answer is this: to have healthy friendships, you must be a spiritually and emotionally healthy person yourself. Only then will you attract and sustain positive friendships.

infuse (in FYOOZ) ; to cause to be permeated with something (as a principle or quality) that alters usually for the better

Here's an easy way to remember the characteristics of a healthy **FRIEND:**

Faithful to us

Roles

Impacts us

Essential

Needs to be nurtured

Dares to hold you accountable

Faithful: Healthy friendships are faithful friendships. Remember, whoever is a constant gossip *to* you will also be a gossip *about* you.[6] A true friend will stand by you when no one else does. He or she will continually believe the best about you and call you to a higher standard. Jesus showed this when He continued to love and believe in Simon Peter, even though He knew Peter would one day deny Him. He said to Peter, "Simon, Simon! Indeed, Satan has asked for you, that he may sift you as wheat. But I have prayed for you, that your faith should not fail; and when you have returned to Me, strengthen your brethren" (Luke 22:31–32). Jesus knew that Peter would betray Him, yet He said, "I am praying for you."

GROUP DISCUSSION:

How would you define a "true" friend?

Are you a true friend?

Do you have true friends?

Roles: Healthy friendships involve various roles. If you don't make friends with people who are different from you in their interests, beliefs, and culture, then you will probably find yourself pretty lonely. It's not always about whether you're simply friendly, it's about how much time and influence you allow that person.

Meet lots of people, but choose their place in your life carefully. Look at how Jesus did it:

+ *Intimate friends*—Jesus's disciples walked with Him daily, sharing every struggle, fear, and triumph. They were by His side during his three years of ministry, and they rejoiced when He rose again. He shared His deepest thoughts with them, and their thoughts were important to Him as well.

+ *Close, personal relationships with giving people*— Jesus didn't get to see Mary, Martha, and Lazarus often, but when He did, they had a great friendship. Martha made huge feasts of food when Jesus traveled to visit. We know Jesus was poor and had no home of His own, so He probably appreciated this act of friendship. Mary was a great listener, and this so blessed Jesus that He proclaimed her gift as "that good part" (Luke 10:42). The Scripture says that Jesus loved Lazarus as a dear friend. They were both believers and had a great time hanging out together.

> A true friend doesn't run out the door at the first sign of conflict.

+ *Acquaintances*—Jesus loved people and stopped to talk, heal, and enjoy conversation as He walked through the crowds. He was a great listener as well as a speaker. Jesus was friendly whether people believed in Him or not, but He was selective about whom He spent intimate time with.

Ask yourself, "How do my friendships affect my daily choices?" List some influences below:

Friend's Name	Resulting Action

What I wear?

What or whom I listen to?

Where I hang out?

What I do with free time?

Which of my friends will likely influence me in a good or bad way this week?

Impacts us: Friendships inevitably impact our lives. Healthy friendships will encourage us to develop healthy attitudes and behaviors, while unhealthy friendships can influence us to develop unhealthy ones. It's a natural law that we become like the people we surround ourselves with. As 1 Corinthians 15:33 says, "Do not be deceived: Evil company corrupts good habits."

The police define a *gang* as a group of individuals who associate on a continuous basis, form an allegiance for a common purpose, and are involved in delinquent or criminal activity.[7] Gang members can be identified by their colors, symbols, and slogans. Their appearance and mannerisms help to affiliate them.

People with positive attitudes don't hang out with people who spend life complaining. Gossips run with other gossips who will listen to their garbage.

What attitude are you attracting?

_____

_____

_____

Why do you think that is?

_____

_____

_____

diffuse (di FYOOZ) : to pour out and permit or cause to spread freely; to extend, scatter

Proverbs 18:24 states, "A man that has friends must himself be friendly." Do you think that you could do more to make friends, to be a friend, or to promote new friendships?

①

What ONE THING would help you to have healthier and happier friendships?

_____

_____

Essential: Healthy friendships are essential in our lives. It has been God's plan from the beginning that we would enjoy friendships. When He created the world, God said, "It is good" (Genesis 1:31). But when God created Adam, He said, "It is not good that man should be alone" (Genesis 2:18). Notice that God did not say, "It is not good for man to be unmarried." He said "alone," meaning that He intended for us to enjoy good relationships, including a growing, healthy relationship with Himself. That's why loneliness is such a powerful downer in our lives. We just weren't made to exist without relationships.

> Those closest to you will determine your success.
> —John Maxwell

The importance of friendship to our emotional well-being is what makes cliques in our youth group so damaging. Think about how great a good friendship can make you feel—one in which you experience support, joy, love, comfort, and encouragement. But how do you feel when you are socially "shut out"? Whether it is intentional or unintentional, you feel the opposite—lonely, misunderstood, and unloved.

When we include others and are unconditionally friendly—particularly to those who might be a bit more difficult to love or who seem unfriendly—we are most effectively showing who Jesus is to a world who doesn't know Him.

By showing myself friendly and being an encourager to others, I can share Christ and His love. I do not have to choose the lost or negative person as an intimate friend, but I can impact that acquaintance by my words and actions.

Needs to be nurtured: Healthy friendships need to be nurtured. It's about being willing to serve and care about people, about being a friend before demanding friendship. When you give friendship, you get it. That's one of God's laws.

Dares to hold you accountable: Leaders surround themselves with accountable and positive friends who dare to hold them accountable.

One day Jesus was passing through a town, and He began talking with a woman (John 4:7–24). She had been married five times and was now living with a man who was not her husband. Because they cared about Jesus and knew the woman's reputation, the disciples questioned whether He should be speaking with her. Of course, we know that Christ's motive was pure. He cared about her and showed her eternal life, but the accountability the disciples wanted was also pure. They were concerned for His reputation and possibly about Him being tempted. But Jesus didn't get angry with the disciples for questioning Him. Instead, He explained to them that He was telling her about salvation.

> *A friend loves at all times, and a brother is born for adversity.*
> —Proverbs 17:17

Just because your friends question one of your actions doesn't necessarily mean they are criticizing you. Paul wrote in Ephesians that as Christians we should be "speaking the truth in love" (4:15).

Accountability sometimes requires forgiving. An awesome story about true friendship is shown in Peter and Jesus. You know about Peter denying Christ, but did you know that after Jesus rose from the dead, He came and found Peter and cooked breakfast for him? He came whether Peter deserved it or not. This one unselfish act showed Peter what a true **FRIEND** looked like.

Christ expects us to forgive as we have been forgiven. This is unconditional and not dependent on feelings, intention, or circumstances. When you approach a friend who might be in trouble, make sure your words are motivated by love.

How will I follow Christ's example of forgiveness and show others the true love of God?

_____

_____

_____

_____

Is there a friend you need to confront in love this week? What will you say? What Scripture can you base this on? Be sure it is not opinion, but truth that motivates you.

_____

_____

_____

_____

_____

_____

_____

_____

[FUSE BOX]

When we feel alone and insecure, we tend to make bad choices, including choosing friends who don't expect much of us spiritually or morally.

> Friendship is born at that moment when one person says to another: "What! You, too? Thought I was the only one."
> —C. S. Lewis

PRIVATE WORLD DEVOTIONS

MONDAY: See it. Read the surrounding passages or chapter for the Key Scripture so that you can get an understanding of the background and context. This helps you to really *see* the verse.

TUESDAY: Hear it. Read the daily Key Scripture and/or surrounding passage out loud, putting your name in, if applicable. For example, John *can do all things through Christ. Thieves have come to destroy* John*, but Jesus has come that* John *might have eternal life.*

WEDNESDAY: Write it. Write the verse and then what it says about:

- ✦ *Others:* Respond, serve, and love as Jesus would.
- ✦ *Me:* Specific attitudes, choices, or habits.
- ✦ *God:* His love, mercy, holiness, peace, joy, etc.

PRIVATE WORLD JOURNAL

I am grateful for—I praise you for—I am feeling—I am thinking—I need help with

PRIVATE WORLD DEVOTIONS *(Continued)*

THURSDAY: Memorize it. Take the verse with you—write it on a card or put it in your phone, iPod, or PDA. Go over it throughout the day so that it begins to *live* in your heart and mind.

FRIDAY: Pray it. Personalize the verse as you pray for yourself or for others or in praise to God. To pray is literally "to think about." Try thinking out loud or writing in your **PRIVATE WORLD JOURNAL.**

SATURDAY: Share it. Ask the Lord to bring someone to mind or in your path today who needs good news. Don't be shy—just let it out! Whether you IM, write, text, tell, or send it, the joy of God's Word will flow from your heart into theirs.

PRAYER REQUESTS

Date	Name	Need	Answer

PRIVATE WORLD JOURNAL

I am grateful for—I praise you for—I am feeling—I am thinking—I need help with

NOTES

CHAPTER 3

I CAN'T REMEMBER
THE BEHAVIOR DRIVEN BY ALCOHOL AND DRUGS

KEY SCRIPTURE

Be sober, be vigilant; because your adversary the devil walks about like a roaring lion, seeking whom he may devour.
—1 Peter 5:8

COULD THIS BE YOU?

Her Side: Max and I were friends for two years, going to parties together and watching out for each other. Our relationship was never physical, but that night something changed. I must have passed out, because all I remember is waking up shivering on the cold bathroom floor. My clothes were all over the place, and I just wanted to go home. I remembered giving in to the drinking, then laughing, and then Max and I kissing—but don't remember anything after that. Those thoughts haunted me day and night. A few weeks later, I started feeling sick, and I was sure it was stress and guilt. It got worse, and I knew I had to talk to my mom. She took me to the doctor, who told me I was pregnant. I tried telling Mom and the doctor that I hadn't had sex, that I was a virgin, but the new life in my body said otherwise. The awful truth, whether I ever remember or not, is that I did have sex with Max that night.

His Side: My friends kept giving me a hard time about hooking up with Allison. One of them gave me a small pill and said, "Use this, and she won't even know it happened." I was nervous, but the more I drank, the more I liked the idea. The pill started to work, and I remember we were laughing and at the time I thought she was OK with it all. I planned to apologize the next day and hoped she wouldn't remember anyway. But there was no second chance. Now my best friend is pregnant and hates me. I will begin paying child support during high school. The friends I was trying to impress don't talk to me anymore, and my parents are hurt beyond words. That one stupid dare changed my life forever.

WHY KNOW IT?

✦ Sometimes called "the forget pill" or "roofie," rophynol is virtually odorless and undetectable. It creates a sleepy, relaxed, and drunk feeling that lasts two to eight hours. Other effects may include blackouts, with a complete loss of memory, dizziness and disorientation, nausea, difficulty with motor movements, and speaking.[1]

✦ 84 percent of women who were date raped knew their attacker.[2]

✦ 90 percent of date rapes occur when either the victim or attacker was drinking.[3]

✦ Nearly 50 percent of U.S. jail and prison inmates were under the influence of alcohol at the time of their offense, and many report not remembering the crime they committed because they were high at the time.[4]

transfuse (trans FYOOZ): to cause to pass from one to another; transmit

Satan's goal is to cause you to make the wrong choices. When you do this, you pay the consequences, but he walks away laughing.

Try picking up one end of a stick. Notice that when you do this, you always end up picking up both ends of the stick, no matter how hard you try not to. Choices are the same way. Every choice leads to a consequence—there are no exceptions.

Be sober, be vigilant; because your adversary
the devil walks about like a roaring lion,
seeking whom he may devour. —**1 Peter 5:8**

In this verse, the apostle Peter warns that Satan attacks on all sides threatening the body, soul, mind, and spirit. Peter was probably describing in this verse the lions used to kill Christians in Roman arenas under the reign of Nero.[5] The fierce beasts put on a show for thousands of spectators who came to watch the roaring lions tear Christians from limb to limb in a disgusting and torturous event. This graphic but true reference gives us a clear mental picture of Satan's violent and insatiable thirst for prey.

infuse (in FYOOZ)*,* to cause to be permeated with something (as a principle or quality) that alters usually for the better

The attacks of Satan, our "adversary," rage in three areas:

1. The battle for the mind

2. The battle for the body

3. The battle for the family

Battle for the Mind: "Be sober" literally means to have a sound and healthy mind, to guard with a wall. It is to "watch, and be mindful."[6] In other words, *pay attention to what you allow into your mind!*

When you use alcohol and other drugs, you open the gate to psychiatric problems such as depression, anxiety, oppositional defiant disorder, and antisocial personality disorder. Why? Consider the following facts:

✦ Alcohol is a mood-altering depressant drug that produces a "who cares, it doesn't matter" state of mind.

✦ Alcohol in large doses, or "binge drinking," can lead to blackouts. As Dr. Robin Smith reported, "I call it dead girl walking syndrome, which means you're not dead yet, but you're killing yourself off. Slowly each time you black out, you're killing off possibilities. You're killing off all that you want to be. You're scared that maybe you can't do it. . . . And do you know what's even more dangerous? Every time you drink, you've got to drink more because the hunger gets bigger and deeper and wider."[7]

When God asks us to "be sober," it is because of His great love for us. He is concerned with what we do and who we are becoming. What does this say about His love for you?

Battle for the Body: Once you lose the battle for the mind, it is easy to lose the battle for the body. "Be vigilant" refers to one who is morally alert. As John Wesley noted, "It is as if he [Peter] had said, Awake, and keep awake. Sleep no more."[8]

Sleepwalking through life is the surest way to lose the battle. What Peter is saying to us is that making a one-time stand against alcohol, drugs, and related sexual behavior is not enough. You have to stay on guard, awake, ready to do battle every day of the journey. There is no vaccination against substance abuse because the struggle is presented to you in a different way and by different people all through life. One way to stay awake is to make the daily choice not to try or use alcohol or other drugs.

How can you do a better job of "staying awake"? Are there specific changes you need to make?

_____

_____

_____

Alcohol and other drugs weaken our defenses. When our defenses are lowered, the body will act out what is in the mind. When we lose the battle for the mind, we then lose the battle for the body.

What specific areas are you struggling with in the area of sexual temptation?

_____

_____

_____

Do you know others who have struggled and won the battle? If so, how did they do it?

_____

_____

_____

Which is easier—to win or lose the battle with alcohol and drugs? (Think about this carefully, considering what you have to deal with after either choice.)

Battle for the Family: Alcohol and other drug use escalates conflict and lack of trust in the home. It can lead to the breakdown of parent-child, spouse, and sibling relationships.

Satan is your enemy, and he will slander and accuse you and cause conflict in your family in an effort to tear it apart. Bible commentator Matthew Henry described Satan as "a roaring lion, hungry, fierce, strong, and cruel, the fierce and greedy pursuer of souls. He walks about, seeking whom he may devour; his whole design is to devour and destroy souls. To this end he is unwearied and restless in his malicious endeavors; for he always, night and day, goes about studying and contriving whom he may ensnare."[9] Don't help Satan by making casual decisions or breaking trust with your parents.

diffuse (di FYOOZ); to pour out and permit or cause to spread freely; to extend, scatter

Satan is a "prowling lion" that roars in an attempt to separate the young from the protection of their parents. If a teen runs ahead or falls behind the protection and care of the family, then that teen becomes easy prey. God's plan is that the family nurtures, encourages, and cares for each other. When the family breaks down, so does God's protection for you. Satan knows this, and he delights in family conflicts.

How can you build trust within your family?

What is ONE THING you can do to improve the communication between you and your parents this week?

Substance abuse violates family trust, can become a financial burden (for example: abuser steals from family, family pays for treatment), and increases the instances of violence within the family. Not only is the parent-child relationship affected, but the relationships between spouses and the relationships between various family members can easily become strained as well.

You may be asking, "But what about 'responsible drinking'?" According to Scripture, there is no such thing.

+ In John 2:9, Jesus turned the water into *oinos* (wine). The Greek word *oinos*, which means wine, is spoken of differently during the days of Jesus than it is today. *Oinos* is a general word that simply refers to the naturally fermented juice of the grape. It was made into a grape juice–like syrup and then watered down to be served at the table. Mixed at a ratio of two parts wine to three parts water, the drink had little alcoholic content.

+ The wine of the Bible was also used as a medicine— both an antiseptic and to settle the stomach. (See Luke 10:30–37, where the good Samaritan poured oil and wine on the man's wounds.) In 1 Timothy 5:23, Paul encourages Timothy to "use [not drink] a little wine for your stomach's sake and your frequent infirmities."

GROUP DISCUSSION

+ Ephesians 5:18: "And do not be drunk with wine, in which is dissipation [wasteful living]." Notice the command—"Do not." Doesn't leave much room for discussion, does it?

+ Proverbs 20:1: "Wine is a mocker, strong drink is a brawler, and whoever is led astray by it is not wise." What kind of present-day situations might apply to this verse?

+ Romans 12:1–2: "Present your body . . . holy . . . acceptable to God. . . . Be transformed by the renewing of your mind." Can you present a holy body and a transformed mind to God if you are using alcohol or other drugs?

◆ Romans 14:21: "It is good neither to eat meat nor drink wine nor do anything by which your brother stumbles or is offended or is made weak." What if by drinking alcohol you cause someone else to drink and their drinking results in crime, bodily harm, or addiction? What is your responsibility as a Christian leader?

It's clear in Scripture what the will of God is concerning alcohol. Don't play the game.

Now that you understand what the Scripture says about alcohol, how do you share that with others without appearing judgmental?

_____

_____

_____

_____

How will your decision about drinking affect your ability to share your faith? Will it help or hurt?

_____

_____

_____

Adversary: one who contends with, opposes, or resists; an enemy; having or involving antagonistic parties or opposing interests; an opponent in a lawsuit.

FUSE BOX

A decision made under the influence of alcohol or other drugs carries with it a consequence that lasts forever.

NOTES

> I never use alcohol because I don't want anything or anyone controlling or making choices for me.
> —Pat Williams, Sr. VP of the NBA's Orlando Magic

PRIVATE WORLD DEVOTIONS

MONDAY: See it. Read the surrounding passages or chapter for the Key Scripture so that you can get an understanding of the background and context. This helps you to really *see* the verse.

TUESDAY: Hear it. Read the daily Key Scripture and/or surrounding passage out loud, putting your name in, if applicable. For example, <u>John</u> *can do all things through Christ. Thieves have come to destroy* <u>John</u>*, but Jesus has come that* <u>John</u> *might have eternal life.*

WEDNESDAY: Write it. Write the verse and then what it says about:

✦ *Others:* Respond, serve, and love as Jesus would.

✦ *Me:* Specific attitudes, choices, or habits.

✦ *God:* His love, mercy, holiness, peace, joy, etc.

PRIVATE WORLD JOURNAL

*I am grateful for—I praise you for—I am
feeling—I am thinking—I need help with*

PRIVATE WORLD DEVOTIONS *(Continued)*

THURSDAY: Memorize it. Take the verse with you—write it on a card or put it in your phone, iPod, or PDA. Go over it throughout the day so that it begins to *live* in your heart and mind.

FRIDAY: Pray it. Personalize the verse as you pray for yourself or for others or in praise to God. To pray is literally "to think about." Try thinking out loud or writing in your **PRIVATE WORLD JOURNAL.**

SATURDAY: Share it. Ask the Lord to bring someone to mind or in your path today who needs good news. Don't be shy—just let it out! Whether you IM, write, text, tell, or send it, the joy of God's Word will flow from your heart into theirs.

PRAYER REQUESTS

Date	Name	Need	Answer

PRIVATE WORLD JOURNAL

I am grateful for—I praise you for—I am feeling—I am thinking—I need help with

NOTES

I ALREADY BLEW IT

ROBBED BY THE PAST

KEY SCRIPTURE

Therefore, if anyone is in Christ, he is a new creation; old things have passed away; behold, all things have become new.

—2 Corinthians 5:17

COULD THIS BE YOU?

The day my dad drove off with another woman was the day my life began to spiral downward. In my mother's home, I felt alone and abandoned, and I experienced the consequences of my parents' bad decisions. New stepdads and boyfriends came and went, and each one brought new abuse into the home. I was beaten and cursed by these men, and I was sexually abused by a temporary stepbrother.

At the age of twelve, I decided that any crowd would be better than the one in my home. I left and began a dangerous life involving drugs and alcohol. The pain and shame of my childhood cut so deeply that nothing else seemed to faze me. By the age of thirteen, I had already spent time in detention centers and in jail.

> You are only a victim once; after that you are a volunteer.
> —Wynona Judd

I kept trying to drown my problems in alcohol, but I found out that my problems could swim! My next drug of choice was speed, which I shot up frequently. I dropped out of school, telling everyone it was "useless." I also gave up on life, choosing to get high at every opportunity to avoid the day altogether. I started to believe what everybody was saying to be true: "Jay, you'll never be anything but bad news."

WHY KNOW IT?

✦ 30 percent of students in America will not complete high school. From 1990 to 2000, the high school completion rate declined in all but seven states; and in 2000, it was only at 69.9 percent.[1]

✦ 33 percent of girls who become pregnant during high school will not graduate, and 80 percent will end up on welfare.[2]

✦ An estimated 5,000 adolescents in America will commit suicide this year.[3]

✦ Depression, a treatable disorder, plays a role in 76 percent of child and teen suicides.[4]

✦ 8 million Americans who were active churchgoers as teenagers are no longer active in church by their thirtieth birthday.[5]

transfuse (trans FYOOZ); to cause to pass from one to another; transmit

Many of us are the victims of abandonment, betrayal, and hurt. These feelings may have been caused by childhood or just everyday life, from those close to us or those we barely know. The hurt they leave behind is real and affects how we think, what our relationships are like, and how we live in the future.

If we aren't careful, that hurt can take us from being *victims* into being *villains*. We deal with our pain by hurting others with actions or with words, and we replace good choices with risky behavior and an "I don't care" attitude. It's important to remember your hurt is very real. Talk to a trusted friend or counselor about how to start your journey to healing.

When we are too embarrassed to get help, or when we just simply choose to stay in an unhealthy state of mind, we allow sin to rule our lives and we become a *volunteer*, rather than a victim. The underlying issue is our lack of confidence in God to be able to heal us and a fear of facing the pain.

And He died for all, that those who live should live no longer for themselves, but for Him who died for them and rose again. Therefore, from now on, we regard no one according to the flesh. Even though we have known Christ according to the flesh, yet now we know Him thus no longer. Therefore, if anyone is in Christ, he is a new creation; old things have passed away; behold, all things have become new. **—2 Corinthians 5:15–17**

When you accept Christ as your Savior, you are now "in Christ." He is no longer just an outward god that you know about—He is the Savior of your soul who lives within you! Because of this, you receive a new life and the power to live it successfully.

infuse (in FYOOZ)¦ to cause to be permeated with something (as a principle or quality) that alters usually for the better

The life we want to live is one of triumph over the pain of the past, whether it was fifteen years ago or yesterday. That victory is available in Christ, but we must make a conscious, definite choice to accept it by faith. First John 5:4 says, "For whatever is born of God overcomes the world. And this is the victory that has overcome the world—our faith."

A lack of faith is actually a lack of confidence in God. God is patient with you, and He has made a way for you to find great power in believing.

There are **four myths** about the past that will rob you of the powerful, peaceful identity Christ intends for you as His child.

> Behold—The present, visible, undeniable change! All things are become new: new life, new senses, new faculties, new affections, new appetites, new ideas and conceptions.
>
> —John Wesley

Myth #1: "My past is a mess. I have nothing to live for."

Truth: God provides you with a **new purpose in life.** Scripture tells us that Jesus "died for all, that those who live should live no longer for themselves, but for Him who died for them and rose again" (2 Corinthians 5:15). When you no longer live for yourself, you leave behind the bitterness, hurt, and the grip of the past. Focus on this: Christ rose from the dead. When He did, He proclaimed His victory over death, sin, and the pain of the past. When you receive Him, you have access to the same power that raised Him from the dead. That's huge!

When you don't accept the truth about God's complete forgiveness of your sin and past, then you allow the thief of the past to rob you of the abundant life Christ wants you to have. But what should you do about the past? You can't pretend it didn't happen. You can't undo it. But you can choose not to live for it.

When you put the past behind you and change your attitude in the present, you begin to walk in a hopeful future. What's your choice today?

If you believe that Christ died on the cross for all sin, then does that mean you can be forgiven for bad choices in the past?

_____

_____

_____

When Christ died on the cross, He said, "It is finished" (John 19:30). What was finished?

_____

_____

_____

We know that the apostle Paul, who was once called Saul, persecuted and murdered Christians before God revealed Himself to Paul. With these past mistakes weighing on his mind, he wrote, "Brethren, I do not count myself to have apprehended; but one thing I do, forgetting those things which are behind and reaching forward to those things which are ahead, I press toward the goal for the prize of the upward call of God in Christ Jesus" (Philippians 3:13–14).

Paul chose to focus on the future, not on the past. What will you focus on?

_____

_____

_____

If you allow the past to dominate your thought life, what risks might that produce for your future?

_____

_____

_____

Myth #2: "I can't help it. It's not my fault. You don't know what I went through."

Truth: In Christ, you are a "**new creation**" (2 Corinthians 5:15), *so stop making excuses.* Some people never shake off the past, and they use it as an excuse to continue making bad choices. They hope their excuse will lessen their feeling of guilt, but instead the guilt continues to build.

Yes, it is true that we are deeply affected by both the successes and failures of our lives, but there comes a time when we must grow up emotionally. We can no longer use our mistakes or the actions of others as a reason for our inability to live strong and true lives. Christ most certainly can make you a godly, peaceful teen. When you receive Christ as your personal Savior, you no longer live in the flesh—that is, you value others and yourself in a new way. You are no longer bound by old habits, family traits, or by your own personality and limitations. Now you have His power. You are commanded to love yourself as He loves you—unconditionally, without regard to past mistakes. When we get this, we get a fresh wind in our sails and a new start in our hearts.

> Don't crucify your today between the two thieves of yesterday and tomorrow.

diffuse (di FYOOZ); to pour out and permit or cause to spread freely; to extend, scatter

Myth #3: "I've made too many mistakes. My past is a mess. Everyone says I won't ever be anything but a failure."

Truth: In Christ, you are the owner of a **new potential**. Let's quit playing games and get to the heart of the matter. *This transformation is the main thing that distinguishes being a Christian from any other religion.* It's not just rules to live by or a set of doctrines. There is a dynamic truth that Jesus Christ is alive—that He rose from the dead. Because of this, Christ now focuses on your future. Your future does not depend on what you think you can achieve or even on what others think about you. Instead, it is built upon the power of Christ to do "exceedingly abundantly above all that we ask or think." Most importantly, it is "according to the power that works in us" (Ephesians 3:20). What power is that? The same power that raised Christ from the dead.

Imagine that you own an entire shopping mall, but you have no keys to any of the stores. You need shoes, health and beauty supplies, and clothes—all of which are yours, but you can't get to any of them. Compare this to Christ offering you the potential to be able to "do all things through Christ who strengthens

> Remember when Peter denied Jesus three times in public? He went on to write two books of the Bible, preach the gospel in many countries, and then died as a martyr because he would not give up presenting the message of Christ. God changed Peter's life. And He will do it for you.

me" (Philippians 4:13), yet you continue to live as you do.

List below ONE THING you would like to do for Christ but feel your past keeps you from doing.

_____

_____

_____

Don't miss this! When you read in 2 Corinthians 5:17 that "if anyone is in Christ, he is a new creation," it describes a miracle that only God can do in your life—give you salvation, new life, forgiveness of sins, and victory over the past and death. These miracles are *exclusive* to Him; you cannot receive them any other way.

> **Faith sometimes begins by stuffing cotton in your ears.**
> —Max Lucado, *He Still Moves Stones*

The Genesis story tells us that God made man out of the dust of the earth just because He wanted to. He can also make you a brand-new creation out of the dust of your past just because He loves you enough to want to.

It isn't about trying harder. It's about fully receiving the power of God available to you and allowing Him to heal you by working in you and through you. You must allow God to do for you what you cannot do for yourself.

Still wondering about those weaknesses in your life? Everyone's got them, but only those who have received the power of Christ triumph over them. When an athlete finds a weakness in his body or talent, he sets out to build up that area, to study, and to prepare to be stronger and better. You can do the same by setting new goals of Scripture memory, prayer time, and finding new friends.

 Are you still blaming others or circumstances for the bad choices you made? Decide today to accept responsibility for your past mistakes and to move forward to new habits in the future.

What are the sins of your past that haunt your mind?

_____

_____

_____

Choose ONE THOUGHT that you can replace a past memory with. For example, when you think of sexual sin of the past, replace that thought with a mental picture of Christ smiling at you and encouraging you to go forward with new potential. If you think of anger, replace that with a mental picture of a peaceful stream and focus on good thoughts.

Myth #4: "I've made a mess of my life, and I'm a hypocrite now. God can never use me to help anyone else."

Truth: You can move forward into a **new presentation**. The unconditional love of God means that the past is completely forgiven and forgotten by God. You can start all over again. Yes, it's true that the consequences of our choices follow us, and we have to deal with these. But is your testimony ruined forever because you made bad choices? No way! The love of God is too strong and His forgiveness is too deep for that. "Therefore, since we have this ministry, as we have received mercy, we do not give up" (2 Corinthians 4:1).

GROUP DISCUSSION

Which of these truths do you feel is the least understood in our culture today?

What about in your own life?

You can rebuild your life and your testimony. No matter how much time it takes, rebuilding is always worth the effort. Don't be afraid to start over and present yourself as one who has fallen but risen again to stand tall. By walking in a consistent life, you can help others to forsake the past and move forward in strength.

You have been set free to live in new attitudes and actions. Salvation is exclusive to God, but it is also extensive. Remember, 2 Corinthians 5:17 says that when you are saved, "Old things have passed away." Don't settle for anything less.

How can you present Christ to others in light of a past mistake? Powerfully! Turn something bad into something very good by sharing the good news! This gives you the opportunity to talk about:

- ✦ God's unconditional love
- ✦ His great mercy
- ✦ His death on the cross in payment for sin
- ✦ How to be forgiven

[FUSE BOX]

Because God loves me and has a plan for my life,
I can choose what type of person I will become:
a victim, a villain, a volunteer, or a victor!

And such were some of you. But you were washed, but you were sanctified, but you were justified in the name of the Lord Jesus and by the Spirit of our God.
—1 Corinthians 6:11

PRIVATE WORLD DEVOTIONS

MONDAY: See it. Read the surrounding passages or chapter for the Key Scripture so that you can get an understanding of the background and context. This helps you to really *see* the verse.

TUESDAY: Hear it. Read the daily Key Scripture and/or surrounding passage out loud, putting your name in, if applicable. For example, <u>John</u> *can do all things through Christ. Thieves have come to destroy* <u>John</u>, *but Jesus has come that* <u>John</u> *might have eternal life.*

WEDNESDAY: Write it. Write the verse and then what it says about:

✦ *Others:* Respond, serve, and love as Jesus would.

✦ *Me:* Specific attitudes, choices, or habits.

✦ *God:* His love, mercy, holiness, peace, joy, etc.

PRIVATE WORLD JOURNAL

I am grateful for—I praise you for—I am feeling—I am thinking—I need help with

PRIVATE WORLD DEVOTIONS *(Continued)*

THURSDAY: Memorize it. Take the verse with you—write it on a card or put it in your phone, iPod, or PDA. Go over it throughout the day so that it begins to *live* in your heart and mind.

FRIDAY: Pray it. Personalize the verse as you pray for yourself or for others or in praise to God. To pray is literally "to think about." Try thinking out loud or writing in your **PRIVATE WORLD JOURNAL.**

SATURDAY: Share it. Ask the Lord to bring someone to mind or in your path today who needs good news. Don't be shy—just let it out! Whether you IM, write, text, tell, or send it, the joy of God's Word will flow from your heart into theirs.

PRAYER REQUESTS

Date	Name	Need	Answer

PRIVATE WORLD JOURNAL

I am grateful for—I praise you for—I am feeling—I am thinking—I need help with

NOTES

CHAPTER 5

TOO ASHAMED TO TALK ABOUT IT

SEXUAL SECRETS AND EXPERIMENTS

(We strongly recommend this chapter be taught in separate girl and guy groups.)

KEY SCRIPTURE

Flee also youthful lusts; but pursue righteousness, faith, love, peace with those who call on the Lord out of a pure heart.
—**2 Timothy 2:22**

COULD THIS BE YOU?

A few years ago, people in surrounding communities were shocked to learn that in a growing suburb just east of Atlanta, there had been an outbreak of syphilis among teenagers.

"I felt like I wasn't pretty enough or I wasn't smart enough," stated Amy, one of the teens involved in the outbreak. Amy's dad described her as a joy to be around when she was in elementary school. She wasn't from a broken home. She was active in sports, had lots of friends, and spent time with her family. After being cut from the cheerleading squad in tenth grade, Amy said she felt depressed a lot. "I guess I kind of picked the wrong friends outside of school. They would buy me alcohol, and I was so happy for a little while."

However, Amy's new friends, mostly guys, weren't really that nice to her. Amy admits, "They didn't treat us [she and the other girls] like we were anything real important." But Amy decided that even though they weren't kind to her, being with them was better than being alone.

What started out as casual sexual activity quickly turned into group sex. Girls were passed from guy to guy like a pack of cigarettes. From that small group, the sexual activity resulted in seventeen teenagers testing positive for syphilis. More than two hundred others were exposed and treated, and approximately fifty of those tested admitted to being involved in extreme sexual behavior, having between twenty and one hundred sexual partners. Dr. Kathleen Toomy said that the final chart tracing the sexual activity looked like a "ball of yarn."[1]

WHY KNOW IT?

✦ In a new kind of spin the bottle, students as young as twelve are experimenting with oral sex, lesbianism, homosexuality, and sexual gratification.[2]

✦ Oral sex isn't considered sex by most teens.[3]

✦ For many teenagers, being a "technical virgin" has become an acceptable alternative to abstinence.[4]

transfuse (trans FYOOZ): to cause to pass from one to another; transmit

Remember this about sexual experimentation: *no one can make you do it.* You have a built-in compass that says, "Don't." You might feel like everyone is doing it, but when the consequences come down, you will have to deal with them alone. The choice to be sexually active before marriage crosses the line of everything you believe as a Christian. To think you can experiment and no one will know, or that you can try something sexually and not have it change you, is to deny the truth. People talk, and people will know. And every time you say yes to sin, you are changed. Guilt and shame do that. End of discussion.

Can a man take fire to his bosom, and his clothes not be burned? Can one walk on hot coals, and his feet not be seared? **—Proverbs 6:26–27**

Sexual experimentation is the same as playing with fire—it will burn you and scar you for life. According to Bible commentator Matthew Henry, "The bold presumptuous sinner says, 'I may venture upon the sin and yet escape the punishment; I shall have peace though I go on.' He might as well say, 'I will take fire into my bosom and not burn my clothes, or I will go upon hot coals and not burn my feet.' The fire of lust kindles the fire of hell. It ruins the reputation and entails perpetual infamy upon that."[5]

> If it involves a sex organ, it's sex!
> —Dr. Phil McGraw

The U.S. Fire Administration has this advice on their Web site: PREPARE. PRACTICE. PREVENT THE UNTHINKABLE.[6] That's good advice for life, don't you think? According to this Web site, every day Americans experience the horror of fire, but most people don't understand fire. Similarly, statistics demonstrate that every day many students throw their lives away by sexual experimentation because they didn't pay attention to what they were getting into.

infuse (in FYOOZ)¦ to cause to be permeated with something
(as a principle or quality) that alters usually for the better

The apostle James describes a kind of LSD that isn't chemical, but just as deadly. It is the progression of **L**ust to **S**in to **D**eath: "But each one is tempted when he is drawn away by his own desires and enticed. Then, when desire has conceived, it gives birth to sin; and sin, when it is full-grown, brings forth death" (James 1:14–15).

These verses banish the excuse "Satan made me do it!" Instead, Scripture tells us that the temptation—literally, "the enticing"—comes about through our own desires. In the scriptures, the devil is called "the tempter" (Matthew 4:3); but neither the devil nor any other person or thing is to be blamed so as to excuse ourselves, for the true origin of evil and temptation is in our own hearts.[7]

The source of temptation is from within a person; it is his own evil desire, lust, or inner craving. Those lusts cause us to be baited, dragged away, and entrapped.

Second Timothy 2:22–23 tells us, "Flee also youthful lusts; but pursue righteousness, faith, love, peace with those who call on the Lord out of a pure heart. But avoid foolish and ignorant disputes, knowing that they generate strife."

Note the two calls to action in the above verse:

1. **Flee.** Run away from the situation—literally, "escape" in the Greek. Forget about debating if it's wrong or not that bad. Leave it behind altogether.

2. **Pursue.** In the Latin, this word is *prosequi* (from *pro-*, forward and *sequi*, to follow). The future-tense thinker does not fall into the moment of temptation; instead, he or she actively and en-

ergetically moves forward in life to follow right-eousness, faith, love, and peace.

You cannot allow MTV, the Internet, satellite radio, the Howard Sterns of life, late-night TV porn, or even the guy or girl next-door to devour your future. Think ahead about the tempting situations that you will avoid—or flee!

What or who is the ONE THING I can choose to avoid?

_____

_____

_____

What is the ONE THING I can decide to pursue?

_____

_____

_____

What the culture labels as harmless sexual fantasy actually drives the mind and then causes the body to crave the action of sin. Note that James 1:14 says that we are "drawn away"—away from what? We are drawn away from God's perfect plan, from the protection of the Holy Spirit, from the moral compass that lives within our heart when we belong to Christ.

The Greek phrase translated "drawn away" literally means to entice or to bait, to catch a fish with bait or hunt with snares. This inner craving draws a person out like a fish drawn from its hiding place, and then entices. So a person both builds and baits his own trap.[8]

Notice that the desire is already there. Nothing much has to happen—the crowd control of the culture plants the temptation within your mind, and you fertilize it by choice. When it grows to full size in the mind, then the body acts upon it. This brings forth death to good habits, positive thoughts, and godliness.

GROUP DISCUSSION

If my current habits, hangouts, and friends are putting me in difficult situations, what new steps can I take to change those things?

Name two people you have met or know casually who you could possibly develop a positive, healthy, accountable friendship with:

How can you begin those friendships?

What new goals, habits, or interests could you develop to use your time more wisely?

There is a dirty little secret that is fast becoming public knowledge: many students are too ashamed to tell about their sexual secrets and experiments. Don't play the game of calling yourself a "technical virgin" while you experiment sexually. These one-night stands play for keeps.

Am I guilty of tempting others? Do I need to set limits in my dating life?

Think about it: Are you setting others up for sexual temptation by your words or actions?

Remember that God created sex; He doesn't say that it is wrong. He created it, blessed it, and intended it for your pleasure. Hebrews 13:4 says, "Marriage is honorable among all, and the bed undefiled; but fornicators and adulterers God will judge."

So if you are looking for a ruling on technical virginity, it is simple:

+ That which is done in the marriage bed is blessed of God. That which is done before or outside the marriage bed is cursed of God.

Sexual experimentation causes confusion and will make sexual intimacy with your future spouse significantly more difficult. Open rebellion against God has led to suffering and confusion for many students everywhere. Because of our rebellion against God and His perfect design, we are a generation plagued by sexual experimentation and addictions.

diffuse (di FYOOZ); to pour out and permit or cause to spread freely; to extend, scatter

Fireproofing your life involves preparation of time, mind, heart, body, spirit, and energy. This is no easy task, but it is an essential one.

The U.S. Fire Administration Web site gives excellent information about the danger of fires and how to prevent them.[9] We can take these same tips and apply them to the sexual fire that burns within us and has lasting consequences when we experiment:

+ **Fire is FAST!** There is little time! In less than thirty seconds, a small flame can get completely out of control and turn into a major fire. You know that's right! Decisions made in the heat of the moment determine whether you'll get out unscathed or burned.

+ **Fire is UNEXPECTED!** Most fires occur in the home when people are asleep. The Bible tells us it is high time to awaken out of sleep. Stay alert and don't let the lull of what the crowd does cause you to be off guard.

✦ **Fire is HOT!** Heat is more threatening than flames. A fire's heat alone can kill, and inhaling this superhot air will scorch your lungs or melt clothes to your skin. In five minutes, a room can get so hot that everything in it ignites at once. This is called "flashover." This needs no further explanation!

✦ **Fire is DARK!** Fire starts bright, but it quickly produces black smoke and complete darkness. Sexual experimentation seems like fun at first, but it will darken your soul in a way you can't imagine. The statistics of depression and suicide are alarming for those who play with sex outside of marriage.

> Complete abstinence is easier than perfect moderation.
> —Saint Augustine

✦ **Fire is DEADLY!** Smoke and toxic gases kill more people than flames do. Even if you escape physical consequences, the resulting reputation, shame, and guilt are hard to bear. Don't do it. Don't play with fire!

Living through a fire means taking quick, decisive actions. No one has ever escaped a fire by simply hoping it would go away.

TRY THESE VALUABLE FIRE SAFETY TIPS:

✦ In the event of a fire, remember time is the biggest enemy and every second counts! *Don't let the sexual idea stay in your mind or flirt with the temptation.*

✦ Escape first, and then call for help. *Get out of the room or situation, and then think about the next step.*

✦ Develop a fire escape plan. *Each of us will face sexual temptation at various times in our lives. Make a plan for what you will do and how you will escape before the temptation or situation presents itself.*

✦ Never return to a burning building for any reason; it may cost you your life. *Never go back to a former temptation just to check it out or for any other reason. It won't be any different. It will still call to you, wait for you, and lie to you.*

✦ Finally, having a working alarm dramatically increases your chances of surviving a fire. *Know the Word and have it ready in your mind; have a friend you can call. Don't be burned in the moment.*

Some people tell you just to go with the crowd and do what feels good for you. They say that what you do in private is no one's business, but that's settling for a lie. If someone tells you, "It's no big deal," you need to be ready to show them that God wants to give you the freedom to enjoy all of life, including sexual integrity.

Understand God's Word as it applies to sexual purity, and make your own sexual purity a personal goal. Only then can you explain it to others without sounding judgmental. Only then can you show them that sexual purity is a joyful, worthy goal that provides great satisfaction. Your living testimony will be lifesaving for others as they, too, fight the fires of sexual temptation.

FUSE BOX

You don't have to jump completely into the fire to get burned. Even sexual experimentation harms you emotionally, as well as puts you at risk for STDs.

PRIVATE WORLD DEVOTIONS

MONDAY: See it. Read the surrounding passages or chapter for the Key Scripture so that you can get an understanding of the background and context. This helps you to really *see* the verse.

TUESDAY: Hear it. Read the daily Key Scripture and/or surrounding passage out loud, putting your name in, if applicable. For example, <u>John</u> *can do all things through Christ. Thieves have come to destroy* <u>John</u>, *but Jesus has come that* <u>John</u> *might have eternal life.*

WEDNESDAY: Write it. Write the verse and then what it says about:

✦ *Others:* Respond, serve, and love as Jesus would.

✦ *Me:* Specific attitudes, choices, or habits.

✦ *God:* His love, mercy, holiness, peace, joy, etc.

PRIVATE WORLD JOURNAL

I am grateful for—I praise you for—I am feeling—I am thinking—I need help with

PRIVATE WORLD DEVOTIONS *(Continued)*

THURSDAY: Memorize it. Take the verse with you—write it on a card or put it in your phone, iPod, or PDA. Go over it throughout the day so that it begins to *live* in your heart and mind.

FRIDAY: Pray it. Personalize the verse as you pray for yourself or for others or in praise to God. To pray is literally "to think about." Try thinking out loud or writing in your **PRIVATE WORLD JOURNAL.**

SATURDAY: Share it. Ask the Lord to bring someone to mind or in your path today who needs good news. Don't be shy—just let it out! Whether you IM, write, text, tell, or send it, the joy of God's Word will flow from your heart into theirs.

PRAYER REQUESTS

Date	Name	Need	Answer

PRIVATE WORLD JOURNAL

I am grateful for—I praise you for—I am feeling—I am thinking—I need help with

NOTES

CHAPTER 6

SELF-SABOTAGE
THE HABITS THAT ROB YOUR FUTURE

KEY SCRIPTURE

Finally, my brethren, be strong in the Lord and in the power of His might. Put on the whole armor of God, that you may be able to stand against the wiles of the devil.
—Ephesians 6:10–11

COULD THIS BE YOU?

Charles Robertson, age nineteen, started his day by applying for a loan at Jefferson National Bank. Later that day, he returned to the bank and handed one of the tellers a note demanding money and claiming he had a gun. With money in hand, he ran from the bank. Then he remembered he'd left the note, which was in his handwriting, and he returned to the bank to retrieve it. Now with the money and the note, he ran to his getaway car—only to realize he'd left the keys at the bank. Not wanting to return to the bank again, he hid from police in nearby shops and finally made it home.

> We shape our habits, and then our habits shape us.
> —The Franklin Covey Company

The car he'd left a block from the bank belonged to his roommate. Charles lied and told her the car had been stolen. The roommate quickly called the police to report her stolen car. Minutes later, the police found the roommate's "stolen" car near the bank, tried the keys the forgetful robber had left, and found they fit. The police retrieved Charles's address from the car loan application and drove to his apartment, where he confessed before being taken to the city jail.[1]

Ridiculous? Yes. But sometimes the worst identity thieves are none other than ourselves.

WHY KNOW IT?

✦ The most common forms of self-sabotage are procrastination, overeating, drinking, spending, and acting impulsively without considering the consequences.[2]

transfuse (trans FYOOZ); to cause to pass from one
to another; transmit

Sabotage means deliberate subversion with intent to destroy. While there are many forces that will attempt to rob you of your pure identity as a Christian, the self-sabotage of negative habits is most destructive.

*For this reason we also, since the day we heard
it, do not cease to pray for you, and to ask that
you may be filled with knowledge of His will
in all wisdom and spiritual understanding;
that you may walk worthy of the Lord, fully
pleasing Him, being fruitful in every good
work and increasing in the knowledge of
God; strengthened with all might, according
to His glorious power, for all patience and
longsuffering with joy.* **—Colossians 1:9–11**

The apostle Paul loved the church that he once persecuted. He literally poured out his life for the gospel and wrote letters to the churches in order to teach doctrine, settle arguments, and encourage spiritual growth and evangelism. In the book of Colossians, he addresses many habits of self-sabotage by praying through each one.

Most of us struggle with a consistent prayer life. We can use this powerful template found in the book of Colossians to break bad habits and instill powerful, new habits into our lives. As a result, we will keep our identity sure and strong.

This lesson teaches you how to pray powerfully for yourself! It is not to be taken lightly or rushed through. In fact, keep it in a place where you can refer to it often as you develop a productive, Christ-honoring life.

infuse (in FYOOZ); to cause to be permeated with something (as a principle or quality) that alters usually for the better

Let's look at the destructive habits that cause self-sabotage and the heart changes listed in Colossians 1:9–11 that can banish those habits. You'll find these listed throughout the chapter.

(**SS** = Self-Sabotage Habit; **HC** = Heart Change)

SS: A "take-it-or-leave-it" attitude about prayer. The national debate over whether we are allowed to pray in school or mention prayer on television swings on the emotion of the moment. For example, during a recent hurricane preparation interview, a reporter asked a town mayor what the people should do. He replied, "Pray, pray, pray." When our troops are in trouble, we say, "We are praying for the troops." This is what has become known as "sunshine prayer"—people only talk about prayer when the situation is dark and they need help.

HC: "Do not cease to pray" (v. 9). If you want a powerful prayer life, then you must have a consistent prayer life.

What is a good time for you to set aside to pray earnestly—early in the morning, before bed, or during the day? Set a time, plan it daily, and keep your prayer journal in the same spot so that you can record both requests and answers. It can be ten minutes, an hour, or short prayers throughout the day. The key is consistency and faith.

SS: Living for the next thrill or dare. A self-sabotaging person constantly asks, "What can I buy? Where's the party? Who's online? Where's my cell phone? How can I connect with someone, anyone?"

HC: "You may be filled" (v. 9). Jesus said, "The thief does not come except to steal, and to kill, and to destroy. I have come that they may have life, and that they may have it more abundantly" (John 10:10).

Pray that you will be able to experience nothing less than the abundant life Jesus promised in John 10:10. Focus on enjoying life, learning the value of simple pleasures, appreciating your family and friends, and guarding against being addicted to wastefulness of your time or money.

SS: The "whatever" mentality. "Whatever" was a popular phrase a few years ago. It was printed on T-shirts, used in commercials and movies, and was considered funny. But that is a boring attitude that leads nowhere.

HC: "With the knowledge of His will" (v. 9). When we set goals and walk in the will of God, we are, as this verse teaches in the Greek, "headed in the right direction." Every person must strive to know God's individual plan and purpose for his or her life.

Pray that you will seek God's best and establish good habits. Why settle for what everyone else knows when you can know the will of God?

SS: Just getting by in school. When we lose the joy of learning, we give up. That is the main reason that 30 percent of students in America do not complete high school.[3]

HC: "In all wisdom" (v. 9). Your individual learning style may be different than others', but it does not mean that you cannot have a habit of mental excellence. This wisdom Paul speaks of is the foundation of mental excellence.

diffuse (di FYOOZ) ; to pour out and permit or cause to spread freely; to extend, scatter

Pray for the ability to learn, to have good study skills and habits, good memory, and an excellent relationship with teachers and those in authority.

✦ **What if I have a learning difference?** Statistics show that almost 2.9 million students in the U.S. are classified as having specific learning disabilities.[4] Learning differences happen when people take in or process information incompletely or in a way different than other people. If someone has a learning or communication difference, it does not mean they are dumb or incapable. It may just mean that the person needs to find a different way to learn or to communicate. A person can be of average or above-average intelligence and yet struggle to keep up with people of the same age in learning and regular functioning because of these differences. But there's hope! Remember that you haven't done everything until you've asked for help.

SS: Live on borrowed faith. Students often ride along on the coattails of their parents' faith. God does honor the good choices of your parents and their faith, but this doesn't allow you to coast through life.

HC: "Spiritual understanding" (v. 9). Pray to begin developing spiritual independence so that you will make the transfer from a parent's faith to your own genuine faith in Christ.

Pray that the truth and teachings of Scripture will permeate and rule your life. Use Scripture memorization as a positive tool in your life.

SS: Judge our morality by others instead of the holiness of God. A huge step toward maturity occurs when you no longer look to others for what is right or wrong or what you can get by with, but instead you begin to look at the holiness of God as your measuring stick for behavior.

HC: "That you may walk worthy of the Lord" (v. 10). Pray for responsibility, morality, the understanding of right and wrong, and the overcoming of temptation. Be sure you bring positive people into your life, people of faith who can live strong in difficult days and encourage you.

Think of the choices you made last week or the choices awaiting you in the next few days. Ask yourself, "What would Jesus do? Could I do this if Christ were physically standing in front of me?" What would the answer be?

SS: Focus on pleasing people. The moment you begin to make decisions based on whether people will like you or not is the moment when confusion begins to rule your life. Remember that the person you are concerned about impressing may not even be around in a few months. What if you make a life-altering decision for that guy or girl and they don't even care?

HC: "Fully pleasing Him" (v. 10). The only reliable justification for working hard to please others is when we live to fully please God by *serving* others, not by *impressing* them. Pray that the Lord will give you a meaningful place of service and a love for your church. When we learn to serve, we learn to relate rightly to other people.

Consider being a "time tither." Give 10 percent of your free time to the charitable act of your choice. It might be cleaning a neighbor's house or babysitting someone's children for free, or it might be visiting people at a nursing home, mentoring students, calling others to encourage them, and so on. Be creative in your choices. Creating opportunities for serving with purpose banishes boredom from the present and builds peaceful habits for the future.

SS: Allow failure to rule emotion. Failure can make a great teacher, or you can choose to let it send you to depression and a lesser life without joy and purpose.

HC: "Being fruitful in every good work" (v. 10). Pray to be successful in your endeavors—not to necessarily win every game or score high on every test, but to find an area of life you enjoy doing and can do well in.

If you allow failure to rule your self-image now, it will follow you as an adult. Don't hesitate to share your failures with trustworthy

Jay Leno has worked very hard all his life. A mild dyslexic, he did not do very well in school, getting mainly Cs and Ds. Jay, however, was determined to accomplish his goals. Despite his poor grades, he was determined to attend Emerson College in Boston. While told by the admissions officer that he was not a good candidate, Jay had his heart set on attending the university and sat outside the admission officers' office twelve hours a day, five days a week until he was accepted into the university. Jay credits his dyslexia with enabling him to succeed in comedy. He also credits his dyslexia with helping him develop the drive and perseverance needed to succeed in comedy, and life in general.[5]

people. Ask them to help you move forward and to pray for you.

What is the ONE THING you can learn from a recent failure? (For example, not to be afraid of trying, not to do things because others do it, to find a better way to do something, to plan before starting something, to get help, etc.) Write what you've learned below:

_____

_____

_____

SS: Talk about a god, but don't learn about _The_ God.
Who is God to you? A name, a book, an idea? He most surely is a powerful, personal Savior who created the world and rose from the dead. Concentrate on that.

HC: "Increasing in the knowledge of God" (v. 10). Learn about God's holiness, and your life will be empowered and transformed!

Only when you have faith and confidence in God will you be able to effectively share with others.

SS: Be content to be weak spiritually, emotionally, and physically. When we fall in the habit of only praying, "Don't let me fall; protect me; help me," then we will feel weak and vulnerable. God intends for us to be strong warriors for His name.

HC: "Strengthened with all might" (v. 11). Praying for protection is important, but too often we forget to pray for strength as well.

Pray through Ephesians 6:10–11, substituting your name in each verse. This is the time when you must make your own correct choices in order to win the battle of temptation by saying yes to God's best.

SS: We rebel against authority in our lives. Arguments with parents over privileges and the resulting feelings of rebellion cause teens to want to run into independence. First Samuel 15:23 warns, "Rebellion is as the sin of witchcraft, and stubbornness is as iniquity and idolatry."

HC: "For all patience" (v. 11). Pray for patience with people like your parents, teachers, and those over you in authority. Pray for the capacity to get along with difficult people who might try to crush your spirit. Pray for the ability to deal with the unlovely without becoming irritated, without bitterness, and without retaliation. Developing these kinds of emotional habits will take you far in life.

> Successful living is not for wimps.

Instead of setting a goal of "getting out of the house," set the goal of walking in patience, maturity, and strength. Remember, God has an amazing future for you. Your part is to prepare and be ready. Don't settle for second best because you ran ahead into your own way.

SS: If it feels good, do it. This is not a culture of self-control. T-shirt slogans abound with self-focused titles like "Princess" and "Spoiled." But as a Christian, you know that it's not about you. It's about God and honoring Him.

HC: "Longsuffering with joy" (v. 11). This is a prayer for self-control in sex, emotions, and other choices. It is an amazing picture in the Greek of turning burdens into glory, of a prayer for self-restraint and even-temperedness on a consistent basis and with joy.

When you learn to walk through difficulty with endurance, you learn something amazing.

GROUP DISCUSSION

Allow each person to share ONE THING in the **SS** category that he or she struggles with. Then during a group prayer time, silent or aloud, pray through Ephesians 6:10–11 for the person next to you by using their name in the verse, as follows:

> *Finally, [say the person's name here] be*
> *strong in the Lord and in the power of His*
> *might. Put on the whole armor of God, that*
> *[say the person's name here] may be able*
> *to stand against the wiles of the devil.*

Pray that the students' failures would become valuable lessons for them as well as for the specific **HC** they need.

FUSE BOX

Instead of struggling through haphazardly,
set new habits that will banish the old ones.
Begin the habit of praying through the Scripture
for a life-changing devotional time. As a result,
you will grow strong and keep your identity pure.

PRIVATE WORLD DEVOTIONS

MONDAY: See it. Read the surrounding passages or chapter for the Key Scripture so that you can get an understanding of the background and context. This helps you to really *see* the verse.

TUESDAY: Hear it. Read the daily Key Scripture and/or surrounding passage out loud, putting your name in, if applicable. For example, <u>John</u> *can do all things through Christ. Thieves have come to destroy* <u>John</u>, *but Jesus has come that* <u>John</u> *might have eternal life.*

WEDNESDAY: Write it. Write the verse and then what it says about:

✦ *Others:* Respond, serve, and love as Jesus would.

✦ *Me:* Specific attitudes, choices, or habits.

✦ *God:* His love, mercy, holiness, peace, joy, etc.

PRIVATE WORLD JOURNAL

*I am grateful for—I praise you for—I am
feeling—I am thinking—I need help with*

PRIVATE WORLD DEVOTIONS *(Continued)*

THURSDAY: Memorize it. Take the verse with you—write it on a card or put it in your phone, iPod, or PDA. Go over it throughout the day so that it begins to *live* in your heart and mind.

FRIDAY: Pray it. Personalize the verse as you pray for yourself or for others or in praise to God. To pray is literally "to think about." Try thinking out loud or writing in your **PRIVATE WORLD JOURNAL.**

SATURDAY: Share it. Ask the Lord to bring someone to mind or in your path today who needs good news. Don't be shy—just let it out! Whether you IM, write, text, tell, or send it, the joy of God's Word will flow from your heart into theirs.

PRAYER REQUESTS

Date	Name	Need	Answer

PRIVATE WORLD JOURNAL

I am grateful for—I praise you for—I am feeling—I am thinking—I need help with

NOTES

ALTERED IMAGES
CHANGING WHO YOU ARE TO FIT IN

KEY SCRIPTURE

I beseech you therefore, brethren, by the mercies of God, that you present your bodies a living sacrifice, holy, acceptable to God, which is your reasonable service.
—**Romans 12:1**

COULD THIS BE YOU?

In eighth grade, Gwen's life quickly became an *Alice in Wonderland*–like trip—except her tunnel didn't lead to magical places. Gwen was mesmerized by the bodies and faces of the celebrities she saw in magazines, and she desperately wanted to become popular. So she decided to become friends with Rachel, whom all the guys at school drooled over.

Rachel was more than happy to teach Gwen the tricks of looking and acting "mature." First lesson: how to shoplift. Rachel said that Gwen needed to do this because she could never afford the right clothes, accessories, and makeup based on her allowance. Next lesson: watching her weight by purging, even though she was barely ninety-five pounds. Once her look was right, Rachel let Gwen in on the final lesson: boys. You could tease, but you didn't want to go all the way. Instead, the girls would simply do "favors" for the popular boys from school or the high school guys who paid attention to them.

Gwen should have been excited about her new popularity, but instead she was scared that her parents would find out, and she felt ashamed about the "favors" that guys had started expecting from her.

WHY KNOW IT?

✦ Sixty percent of college students admitted that a celebrity had influenced their attitudes and personal values, including their work ethic and views on morality, in a study conducted by Dr. Susan Boon. Nearly half said that their idol inspired them to pursue activities including acting, sports, becoming a vegetarian, or using marijuana.[1]

✦ Forty-three percent of young people are on some type of diet.[2]

✦ From 2002 to 2003, the number of girls 18 and younger who got breast implants nearly tripled—from 3,872 to 11,326.[3]

---

transfuse (trans FYOOZ): to cause to pass from one to another; transmit

---

What happens to us? We start out the day with good intentions, but somewhere along the way, we get a message that we don't dress right, look right, think fast enough, add to the team, and so on. The messages come from everywhere—the poster in the hallway, the song on the radio, the guy sitting next to you. Rough language and subject matter surround us like uninterrupted white noise, and we begin to think of profanity as common words. And you start to say to yourself, "I've got to change my clothes, my attitude, my vocabulary, and my choices if I'm going to be someone."

Understand this: every single person on earth feels pressure to change at some point. That's OK—as long as you change for the better and for yourself, not for the worse and for everyone else.

*I beseech you therefore, brethren, by the mercies
of God, that you present your bodies a living
sacrifice, holy, acceptable to God, which is
your reasonable service.* —**Romans 12:1**

Each day that you walk the halls at school, watch a movie, listen to a song, or talk to a friend, you are aware of your culture's acceptance of sexual sin, drug use, and profanity. Yet here is a verse that tells you to live differently. In fact, it gives the opportunity for you to present a gift, a living sacrifice to Christ. *This is one opportunity you don't want to miss!*

The term "living sacrifice" is more easily understood when you realize that this gift is alive—it is the surrender of your inner being to God, resulting in a godly lifestyle. This command is for something far more wonderful than normal or average living; it is choosing to be abnormal and above average. Excel in what you are good at. Be healthy, strong, and physically fit, but remember that God lives within you.

infuse (in FYOOZ) : to cause to be permeated with something (as a principle or quality) that alters usually for the better

Romans 12:2 tells us, "Do not be conformed…but be transformed." Simple message—confusing choices. *Conformed* means to go along with the crowd, to become whatever the color or attitude is of the crowd around you. It's an easy, automatic response by our sinful nature.

Transformed, on the other hand, speaks of radical change by leaving behind one set of influences and choosing another instead. In the Greek, it is the word *metamorphoomai,* which has given us the English word *metamorphosis,* like when a tadpole becomes a frog or a caterpillar becomes a butterfly. In the English language, *trans-* means to carry across, as in *transatlantic.* To transform then, is when we are carried across into something entirely different.

 Before you can present your body holy and acceptable to God, you have to yield your mind and heart to His will. God doesn't really want your flesh; He wants you. The power to *present your body* comes from the choice to *program your mind.*

 The Internet virus Slammer Worm launched on January 25, 2003. In that attack, the first victim was struck at 12:30 a.m. By 12:45, the worm had spread so extensively that large portions of the Internet were failing under the strain. For example, three hundred thousand cable modems in Portugal went dead, and twenty-seven million people in South Korea lost cell phone and Internet service. Flights in Newark were canceled, and 911 dispatchers in Seattle resorted to pencil and paper. The total worldwide damage cost more than $1 billion.[4]

The constant barrage of spam, pop-ups, and unsolicited information that you delete from your computer mailbox also needs to be deleted from the mind. Once you deal with mailbox cleanup, the next step is to install an anti-spyware program. When you program your mind for godliness, you choose to install a firewall in the mind. Renewing the mind through memorizing, reading, writing, meditating, and loving the Word of God gives you protection and power.

 If I want a life that I can present to God, I have to start preparing to be a living sacrifice.

Write ONE THING you can choose that will take you closer to this goal:

_____

_____

_____

_____

Be prepared for what's ahead, and decide in advance to not allow uninvited messages to take control of your brain. Destructive programs come into your computer through "Trojans." They hitch a ride on downloads and messages and look for software vulnerabilities. In a person, there are spiritual and emotional "Trojans" that look for free rides into the mind through media, cultural influences, music, the classroom, and the everyday course of life. Together, these are working to rob you of the peace that God intended you to have.

When you allow the destructive messages of the world to infect your mind, your **PEACE** is replaced by the following:

Pressure

Escape

Availability

Curiosity

Emptiness

Pressure: There are two kinds of destructive pressure that we must face. First, there is outer pressure, or what we call "crowd control." It's the crush of what the culture is promoting at the moment, and it sweeps up the mind through constant messages from the media. From the time you get up in the morning, your mind is barraged by language, ads, photos, and sound bites that you would not choose to hear if you knew they were coming.

According to statistics, the average American, in one year, will read 100 newspapers and 36 magazines, watch 2,463 hours of television, listen to 730 hours of radio, buy 20 CDs, talk on the telephone almost 61 hours, read 3 books, and spend countless hours exchanging information in conversations.[5] We need to pay attention to what's around us and choose beforehand how we will respond.

> There does come a day when the little boy sits down and the man stands up—or the little girl sits down and the woman stands up.

Second, there is inner pressure such as restlessness, boredom, and reactions to current events or home life. The attitude of "anything is better than this" opens the mind to a life of "whatever." Instead of giving in to a "whatever" attitude, choose to hang out with people who are worthy heroes.

Escape: Escape is a reaction to responsibilities and demands on your energy and time that feel like more than you want to handle. Instead of guarding our minds, sometimes we just "check out" mentally. This escape may not take us into a particular sin at first, but it puts our mind in a neutral state and makes us easy prey to the world's destructive messages. Whenever we mentally check out, a new barrage of information and choices tries to check in. These uninvited guests see the vacancy sign from down the road and hurry to drop by.

Availability: It's no secret that destructive substances and behaviors are ready and available anytime. You know exactly what we're talking about here—alcohol or almost any other drug you want is available at school, at the mall, or anyplace you hang out, even sometimes at church. And can we talk about sex for a minute? It used to be that girls were the only ones complaining about sexual pressure, but more and more guys are being approached by girls who want sexual experimentation without commitment. The offers for casual sex and "friends with benefits" are way too easy to receive and accept. What's a guy or girl to do? Program your mind to reject these destructive messages.

When Jesus met the woman at the well, instead of being tempted by her loose moral lifestyle, He immediately began to share about how she could receive eternal life. Ask yourself, "How can I change the course of conversation with others like Jesus did?"

Curiosity: All this availability leads to another problem. The more you think about the world's offers, the more you think, *Hmm, maybe I should try it once. I wonder what it's like.* When you program your mind, you won't be led about by your own curiosity. Hey, this isn't Wonderland, and you aren't Alice. The one-time choices you make bring long-lasting consequences for you, your friends, your family, and your relationship with God. When you program your mind for the adventures God has for you, you won't settle for second-rate chemical experiments. These leave you empty, wanting to try more and more thrills, hoping to find one that "feels" good.

Emptiness: The first four mind-altering factors are why many of us get into trouble, but emptiness is the reason some stay there. As Blaise Pascal said, all of us were born with a God-shaped vacuum in our hearts. We can either fill it on purpose with righteousness or it will fill itself with unrighteousness.

GROUP DISCUSSION

Is living a godly life about fighting temptation or preparing the heart and mind? Can it be both? Which one do you spend more time on? Which one should you spend more time on?

diffuse (di FYOOZ) : to pour out and permit or cause to spread freely; to extend, scatter

What can you share that will help others understand that God has a unique adventure for every person? How about starting with John 10:10? Anything personal you can say about that verse?

Why settle for a false peace through chemicals or crowd control when you can have the authentic peace of God and purpose in your life? These mind-altering factors are responsible for our daily behavior, unless we program our mind to stand in strength with the principles and values of Scripture.

When you program your mind, you can begin to prove what you're made of—or, as Romans 12:2 says, you "prove what is that good and acceptable and perfect will of God."

Let's say, for example, that conversations go something like this at your house: "Mom, I'm late and I need money for lunch. Do you know where my books are? Can you wash my jeans for me tonight? Oh, and I forgot to study for a test today and sorry I missed curfew last night, but it wasn't my fault. Gotta go. Bye, Mom!" Later that day: "I don't know why you can't trust me and treat me like an adult. I'm not a child, you know."

True, you don't feel like a child. But the reality is that you do not yet have the full emotional capacity to function as an adult. Consider these facts:

✦ An adolescent's brain is still growing.[6]

✦ The prefrontal cortex acts as the CEO of the brain, controlling planning, working memory, organization, and modulating mood—but this does not mature until about age twenty-one. In the meantime, as teens mature, they can reason better, develop more control over impulses, and make better judgments.[7]

On the bridge from childhood to adulthood, you might get in the wrong lane, stop to watch the boats, hang out, or get scared and turn around for a while. It's OK, because you're on your bridge, and the process of becoming an adult is uniquely timed.

A godly life is not based on what we DON'T do, but rather on what we DO. God's promise is that you can be "transformed," and the result will be "good and acceptable and the will of God." It is a radical, powerful life that steps away from the ideals, methods, and goals of those who do not follow Christ and steps toward the great adventure of God for your life.

[FUSE BOX]

You don't have to alter your image, even if everyone else you know does. You can present your body to God, program your mind toward godliness, and as a result, prove what you're made of.

Write it: "I, _____ (your name), choose today to live in a way that is above average."

Watch, stand fast in the faith, be brave, be strong.
—1 Corinthians 16:13

NOTES

> Only when the body is dominated by the spirit can there be the life which is pleasing to God, and, thus, satisfying to man.
>
> —Donald Grey Barnhouse

PRIVATE WORLD DEVOTIONS

MONDAY: See it. Read the surrounding passages or chapter for the Key Scripture so that you can get an understanding of the background and context. This helps you to really *see* the verse.

TUESDAY: Hear it. Read the daily Key Scripture and/or surrounding passage out loud, putting your name in, if applicable. For example, <u>John</u> *can do all things through Christ. Thieves have come to destroy* <u>John</u>, *but Jesus has come that* <u>John</u> *might have eternal life.*

WEDNESDAY: Write it. Write the verse and then what it says about:

✦ *Others:* Respond, serve, and love as Jesus would.

✦ *Me:* Specific attitudes, choices, or habits.

✦ *God:* His love, mercy, holiness, peace, joy, etc.

PRIVATE WORLD JOURNAL

I am grateful for—I praise you for—I am feeling—I am thinking—I need help with

PRIVATE WORLD DEVOTIONS *(Continued)*

THURSDAY: Memorize it. Take the verse with you—write it on a card or put it in your phone, iPod, or PDA. Go over it throughout the day so that it begins to *live* in your heart and mind.

FRIDAY: Pray it. Personalize the verse as you pray for yourself or for others or in praise to God. To pray is literally "to think about." Try thinking out loud or writing in your **PRIVATE WORLD JOURNAL.**

SATURDAY: Share it. Ask the Lord to bring someone to mind or in your path today who needs good news. Don't be shy—just let it out! Whether you IM, write, text, tell, or send it, the joy of God's Word will flow from your heart into theirs.

PRAYER REQUESTS

Date	Name	Need	Answer

PRIVATE WORLD JOURNAL

I am grateful for—I praise you for—I am feeling—I am thinking—I need help with

NOTES

CHAPTER 8

IT'S NOT MY FAULT

EXCUSES, EXCUSES, EXCUSES

KEY SCRIPTURE

Then Jesus said to them, "A little while longer the light is with you. Walk while you have the light, lest darkness overtake you; he who walks in darkness does not know where he is going."
—**John 12:35**

COULD THIS BE YOU?

It's not my fault . . .

+ that I got a D on the paper. We weren't supposed to ask parents for help!

+ that I'm so angry. My parents got a divorce.

+ that I started drinking. My friends started it.

+ that I didn't walk the dog. He was asleep!

+ that I was late. Sarah's watch wasn't working.

+ that I didn't get my homework done. No one reminded me.

When you have a "no excuses" policy in your life, you strive for excellence and soar into achievement because you attempt to do things right the first time.

♦ that I got in trouble. It was only because I got caught!

And on and on it goes.

WHY KNOW IT?

♦ In 2002, an estimated 2.3 million juvenile arrests were made.[1]

♦ Thirty-four percent of young women become pregnant at least once before they reach the age of 20.[2]

transfuse (trans FYOOZ): to cause to pass from one to another; transmit

Being a student of faith means you have the courage to face your issues, receive forgiveness and grace, and embrace your future. Excuses are usually the result of an emotional self-defense mechanism. They will hold you hostage and kidnap your future if you let them.

Why do people make excuses?

♦ embarrassment over a bad decision

♦ to avoid the consequence of an action

♦ to avoid criticism

♦ a fear of facing failure

♦ to avoid responsibility

♦ laziness or lack of self-control

♦ to avoid confrontation

♦ to avoid conflict

Now the serpent was more cunning than any beast of the field which the Lord God had made. And he said to the woman, "Has God indeed said, 'You shall not eat of every tree of the garden'?" And the woman said to the serpent, "We may eat the fruit of the trees of the garden; but of the fruit of the tree which is in the midst of the garden, God has said, 'You shall not eat it, nor shall you touch it, lest you die.'" Then the serpent said to the woman, "You will not surely die. For God knows that in the day you eat of it your eyes will be opened, and you will be like God, knowing good and evil." So when the woman saw that the tree was good for food, that it was pleasant to the eyes, and a tree desirable to make one wise, she took of its fruit and ate. She also gave to her husband with her, and he ate. Then the eyes of both of them were opened, and they knew that they were naked; and they sewed fig leaves together and made themselves coverings. And they heard the sound of the Lord God walking in the garden in the cool of the day, and Adam and his wife hid themselves from the presence of the Lord God among the trees of the garden. Then the Lord God called to Adam and said to him, "Where are you?" —**Genesis 3:1–9**

Satan is the author of deception. In Genesis 3, he chose the snake as a disguise in front of Eve because it was "more cunning than any beast" (v. 1). He went for the visual, the weird, and the intriguing. This is the first time in Scripture that Satan steps onto the stage of human history, and it is here that we see how skillful and crafty he can be.

No doubt about it: Eve was punked. Satan set her up for a fall with just the right words: "God has said, 'You shall not eat it, nor shall you touch it, lest you die'" (v. 3).

✦ Satan's test was to get Eve to question the authority of God's Word. If the devil could deceive Eve into questioning God's Word, then he could destroy her personal faith and cause her to act out of doubt.

✦ He could cause her to give more honor to his words than God's.

✦ Her actions would then honor Satan as her authority and would therefore attribute worship to him.

Make no mistake: the devil is smart. Satan was thrown from heaven because he wanted to be worshiped above all else, including the Creator. Since he could not succeed and was thrown out of heaven, he now shows up on earth ready to deceive Eve and then Adam.

She took of its fruit and ate. She also gave to her husband with her, and he ate. (v. 6)

It cannot be ignored that it was a conscious act of both Adam and Eve to eat the forbidden fruit. They had been given the freedom of choice and seized the opportunity to betray the One who had provided that freedom in the first place. The decision to sin was theirs and theirs alone. They could not blame their decision on their upbringing, for they had no upbringing. Nor could they attribute the Fall to being a middle child or not receiving the same amount of presents as a sibling one year at Christmas. Nor could they attribute the blame to being born in the wrong era, for this was the first era. They didn't come from an upper-class neighborhood where they were given too much, nor did they come from a neighborhood lower on the socioeconomic scale. They were in Paradise, and they communed with God daily. Their choice to sin could not be blamed on the influence of culture. It was an act of will.

Then the eyes of both of them were opened. (v. 7)

This is the death of innocence and the birth of conscience. Immediately following the choice to disobey God, waves of shame and guilt rushed over Adam and Eve. Their eyes were opened to the fact they had messed up with God, and they now found themselves stamped with disgrace and humiliation. So they attempted to cover their shame and hide from God.

They sewed fig leaves together and made themselves coverings. (v. 7)

What a weak attempt to disguise their willful choice to rebel against God's command. The fig leaves were not only temporary but completely inadequate to cover their sins. It is easy to laugh at Adam and Eve's belief that fig leaves were going to fool God, but it would benefit us to read this narrative as a mirror of our own lives. We also try to cover our sins with excuses and attempt to hide from consequences. The "fig leaf" excuses we offer to God are inadequate, and hiding is a temporary solution. So why haven't we learned from Adam and Eve? Why haven't we learned from our mistakes?

"Where are you?" (v. 9)

God was calling Adam to come forth from the darkness and back into the light where he could see and be seen. This is the question that God asks each of us today. Can we live in His presence with the kinds of choices we have made, or are we held hostage by choosing to attempt to cover our mistakes in a sea of excuses?

To live in the light is to live a lifestyle of frequent, fresh encounters with the risen Lord Jesus. In this walk of light, there is no need for fear or guilt and no need to hide. We rejoice in fellowship with Him.

infuse (in FYOOZ) : to cause to be permeated with something (as a principle or quality) that alters usually for the better

If Satan can deceive an individual into not believing all of God's Word as truth, then he knows that this individual stops being a passionate follower of God. You cannot worship Him if you don't fully believe in Him.

Very few people would say that they worship Satan. However, if we choose to ignore God's truth and believe some dressed-up lie, then not only are we deceived, but we also honor the deceiver.

What is ONE THING about God's Word that you know to be absolute truth?

Ask God to give you an opportunity to share that truth with someone else in an encouraging way.

 How can I avoid allowing yesterday's problems to ruin tomorrow's possibilities?

As a Christian, how can I rise above excuses and step up to the plate of responsibly, owning up to my mistakes?

Immediately after the Fall, God confronted Adam about his sin. Adam blamed Eve, Eve blamed the snake, and God punished them all. Our sin not only affects our fellowship with God, but it also affects our relationships with others. The slippery slope of excuses will eventually lead us to accuse those whom we hold most dear in life and negatively impact our relationships with family, friends, teammates, and so on.

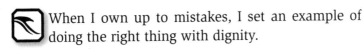
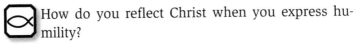

diffuse (di FYOOZ); to pour out and permit or cause to spread freely; to extend, scatter

When I own up to mistakes, I set an example of doing the right thing with dignity.

How do you reflect Christ when you express humility?

When you show people the positive side of a "no excuses" lifestyle, you enable them to walk in truth.

PRIVATE WORLD DEVOTIONS

MONDAY: See it. Read the surrounding passages or chapter for the Key Scripture so that you can get an understanding of the background and context. This helps you to really *see* the verse.

TUESDAY: Hear it. Read the daily Key Scripture and/or surrounding passage out loud, putting your name in, if applicable. For example, <u>John</u> *can do all things through Christ. Thieves have come to destroy* <u>John</u>, *but Jesus has come that* <u>John</u> *might have eternal life.*

WEDNESDAY: Write it. Write the verse and then what it says about:

✦ *Others:* Respond, serve, and love as Jesus would.

✦ *Me:* Specific attitudes, choices, or habits.

✦ *God:* His love, mercy, holiness, peace, joy, etc.

PRIVATE WORLD JOURNAL

I am grateful for—I praise you for—I am feeling—I am thinking—I need help with

PRIVATE WORLD DEVOTIONS *(Continued)*

THURSDAY: Memorize it. Take the verse with you—write it on a card or put it in your phone, iPod, or PDA. Go over it throughout the day so that it begins to *live* in your heart and mind.

FRIDAY: Pray it. Personalize the verse as you pray for yourself or for others or in praise to God. To pray is literally "to think about." Try thinking out loud or writing in your **PRIVATE WORLD JOURNAL.**

SATURDAY: Share it. Ask the Lord to bring someone to mind or in your path today who needs good news. Don't be shy—just let it out! Whether you IM, write, text, tell, or send it, the joy of God's Word will flow from your heart into theirs.

PRAYER REQUESTS

Date	Name	Need	Answer

PRIVATE WORLD JOURNAL

I am grateful for—I praise you for—I am feeling—I am thinking—I need help with

Notes

CHAPTER 1: ID THIEVES AT THE DOOR: THEY COME TO DESTROY

1. Norman Swan, "Frank Abagnale—New Life." Life Matters (17 March 2000). Available at http://www.abc.net.au/rn/talks/lm/stories/s111098.htm (accessed 18 July 2005).

2. "About Frank Abagnale," Abagnale & Associates, www.abagnale. com (accessed 18 July 2005).

3. "Verbal Testimony by Michelle Brown," Privacy Rights Clearinghouse (12 July 2000). Available at http://www.privacyrights.org/cases/victim9.htm (accessed 6 July 2005).

4. Frank Abagnale, "14 Tips to Avoid Identity Theft," *Bankrate* (29 June 2005). Available at http://www.bankrate.com/brm/news/advice/20030124b.asp (accessed 18 July 2005).

5. "Spiritual Development and the College Experience," Higher Education Research Institute UCLA (5 April 2004). Available at http://www.spirituality.ucla.edu/results/analysiscollege.pdf#search = 'change%20religion%20during%20college' (accessed 11 July 2005).

6. "New Religion in America," National Public Radio (13 May 2004). Available at http://www.npr.org/templates/story/story.php?storyId = 1895496 (accessed 11 July 2005).

7. Wade Clark Roof, "Multiple Religious Switching: A Research Note," *Journal for the Scientific Study of Religion* (1999) 28:530–35.

8. "Americans Draw Theological Beliefs From Diverse Points of View," Barna Group (8 October 2002). Available at http://www.barna.org/FlexPage.aspx?Page = BarnaUpdate&BarnaUpdateID = 122 (accessed 11 July 2005).

9. Ibid., (24 September 2003).

CHAPTER 2: LOST IN THE CROWD: THE FORCE OF CULTURE CONTROL

1. J. C. Friday, PhD, "The Psychological Impact of Violence in Under-served Communities," *Journal of Health Care for the Poor and Underserved* 6, no. 4 (1995): 403–409.

2. "Some Things You Should Know About Preventing Teen Suicide," American Academy of Pediatrics. Available at http://www.aap.org/advocacy/childhealthmonth/prevteensuicide.htm (accessed 29 July 2005).

3. Sue Zeidler, "Demand For Pics Swell Paparazzi Ranks," Reuters (29 June 2005). Available at http://xtramsn.co.nz/business/0,,5007-4519546,00.html (accessed 11 July 2005).

4. *Nationwide Newspapers.* http://store.yahoo.com/classifieds/naten.html (accessed 11 July 2005).

5. "Tabloid publicist quits over Diana coverage," *USA Today* (8 July 1999). Available at http://www.usatoday.com/news/diana/diana107.htm (accessed 11 July 2005).

6. Diane Strack, *New Start 4 Single Moms*, Chapter 2: "Healthy Relationships Do Exist," First Orlando Publishing, Orlando, 2004), p 5.

7. "Gangs!" Parents in Crisis. Available at www.geocities.com/Athens/4111/nogangs.html (accessed 11 July 2005).

CHAPTER 3: I CAN'T REMEMBER: THE BEHAVIOR DRIVEN BY ALCOHOL AND DRUGS

1. Data reported in *Catalyst*, National Crime Prevention Council 19, no. 7 (August 2000), based on research by the Bureau of Justice Statistics, the National Institute of Justice, the Center for Substance Abuse Prevention, and the Urban Institute and the Pacific Institute for Research and Evaluation.

2. Ibid.

3. A. Abbey, "Alcohol-Related Sexual Assault: A Common Problem Among College Students," *Journal of Studies on Alcohol* 14 (2002): 118–28.

4. Data reported in *Catalyst*, National Crime Prevention Council 19, no. 7 (August 2000), based on research by the Bureau of Justice Statistics, the National Institute of Justice, the Center for Substance

Abuse Prevention, and the Urban Institute and the Pacific Institute for Research and Evaluation.

5. "Nero," Wikipedia (1 July 2005). Available at http://en.wikipedia. org/wiki/Nero#A_series_of_scandals (accessed on 11 July 2005).

6. Gill, John. "Commentary on 1 Peter 5:8". "John Gill's Exposition of the Bible". http://bible.crosswalk.com/Commentaries/GillsExposi tionoftheBible/gil.cgi?book = 1pe&chapter = 005&verse = 008&next = 009&prev = 007.

7. "Teen Issues: How To Deal," *The Oprah Winfrey Show* (15 April 2005). Available at http://www.oprah.com/relationships/relation-ships_content.jhtml?contentId = con_20050415_teenissues.xml&se ction = Family&subsection = Parenting (accessed on 1 July 2005).

8. Wesley, John. "Commentary on 1 Peter 5". "John Wesley's Explan-atory Notes on the Whole Bible". http://bible.crosswalk.com/ Commentaries/WesleysExplanatoryNotes/wes.cgi?book = 1pe&ch apter = 005.

9. Henry, Matthew. "Commentary on 1 Peter 5". "Matthew Henry Com-plete Commentary on the Whole Bible". http://bible.crosswalk. com/Commentaries/MatthewHenryComplete/mhc-com.cgi?book = 1pe&chapter = 005.

CHAPTER 4: I ALREADY BLEW IT: ROBBED BY THE PAST

1. Paul E. Barton, *"One-Third of a Nation: Rising Dropout Rates and Declining Opportunities,"* Educational Testing Services (February 2005): 3.

2. "General Facts and Stats," The National Campaign to Prevent Teen Pregnancy. Available at http://www.teenpregnancy.org/resources/ data/genlfact.asp (accessed on 1 July 2005).

3. *"Teen Suicide: Student Views of Risks and Protective Factors,"* University of Nevada Corporative Extension, Fact Sheet #89-33. Available at http://www.unce.unr.edu/publications/FS98/FS9833. pdf#search = 'number%20of%20teens%20who%20committed%2 0suicide' (accessed on 2 July 2005).

4. "New UCLA Study Disputes Antidepressant/Suicide Link; Scientists Fear Rise in Deaths From Untreated Depression," *UCLA News* (2 February 2005). Available at http://newsroom.ucla.edu/page. asp?RelNum = 5880 (accessed on 2 July 2005).

5. "Twentysomethings Struggle to Find Their Place in the Christian Church," Barna Group (24 September 2003) Available at http://www.barna.org/FlexPage.aspx?Page = BarnaUpdate&BarnaUpdate ID = 149 (accessed on 11 July 2005).

CHAPTER 5: TOO ASHAMED TO TALK ABOUT IT: SEXUAL SECRETS AND EXPERIMENTS

1. "The Lost Children of Rockdale County." Written by Rachel Dretzin Goodman. Produced and directed by Rachel Dretzin Goodman and Barak Goodman. PBS *Frontline*. 19 October 1999.

2. "A New Kind of Spin the Bottle," *The Oprah Winfrey Show*. (7 May 2002). Available at http://www.oprah.com/tows/pastshows/tows_2002/tows_past_20020507_b.jhtml (accessed on 8 July 2005).

3. "Do You Really Know What Your Teen Is Doing?" *The Oprah Winfrey Show* (2 October 2003). Available at http://www.oprah.com/relationships/relationships_content.jhtml?contentId = con_20031002_slang.xml&section = Family&subsection = Parenting (accessed on 2 July 2005).

4. "Teens, Television, and the Technical Virgin: The Connection Between Viewing Habits and Sexual Behavior," *The Evangelical Outpost* (25 October 2004). Available at http://www.evangelicaloutpost.com/archives/000965.html (accessed on 2 July 2005).

5. Henry, Matthew. "Commentary on Proverbs 6". "Matthew Henry Complete Commentary on the Whole Bible". http://bible.crosswalk.com/Commentaries/MatthewHenryComplete/mhc-com.cgi?book = pr&chapter = 006.

6. FEMA. Available at http://www.usfa.fema.gov/downloads/usfa-parents/Brochure.pdf (accessed on 11 July 2005).

7. Henry, Matthew. "Commentary on Proverbs 6". "Matthew Henry Complete Commentary on the Whole Bible". http://bible.crosswalk.com/Commentaries/MatthewHenryComplete/mhc-com.cgi?book = pr&chapter = 006.

8. J. F. Walvoord and R. B. Zuck, *The Bible Knowledge New Testament Commentary: An Exposition of the Scriptures* (Wheaton, Ill: Victor Books, 1983).

9. "About Fire: The Nature of Fire," USFA (23 November 2004). Available at http://www.usfa.fema.gov/safety/thisis.shtm (accesed on 11 July 2005).

CHAPTER 6: SELF-SABOTAGE: THE HABITS THAT ROB YOUR FUTURE

1. Mike Mather, "Robber Leaves Keys to Getaway Car in Bank," *The Virginian-Pilot* (3 February 1995): B1.

2. Dan Neuharth, "Top 20 Self Sabotaging Behaviors: Secrets You Keep From Yourself." Available at http://www.secretswekeep. com/the_self-sabotage_top_20.htm (accessed on 12 July 2005).

3. Paul E. Barton, *"One-Third of a Nation: Rising Dropout Rates and Declining Opportunities,"* Educational Testing Services (February 2005): 3.

4. "LD at a Glance," National Center for Learning Disabilities (2001). Available at http://www.ld.org/LDInfoZone/InfoZone_FactSheet_ LD.cfm (accessed on 3 July 2005).

5. "Dyslexic? You're Not Alone," Levinson Medical Center for Learning Disabilities (4 April 2003). Available at http://www.dyslexiaonline. com/famous/famous.htm (accessed on 12 July 2005).

CHAPTER 7: ALTERED IMAGES: CHANGING WHO YOU ARE TO FIT IN

1. Courtney Bennett, "Fan Club Confessions: Teens Underestimate Influence of Celebrity Idols," *Psychology Today*, January/February 2002.

2. *True Life: I'm on a Diet.* MTV. Available at http://www.mtv.com/ onair/dyn/truelife/episode.jhtml?episodeID = 90399 (accessed on 4 July 2005).

3. Sandra Boodman, "For More Teenaged Girls, Adult Plastic Surgery," *Washington Post* (26 October 2004): A1.

4. Steve Goll, "Blaster, Spyware, Top Internet Computer Dangers," Steve Goll Consulting (20 August 2003) Available at http://www. stevegoll.com/articles/articles/83.shtml (accessed on 12 July 2005).

5. Joanna M. Burkhardt, Mary C. MacDonald, and Andrée J. Rathemacher, *Teaching Information Literacy: 35 Practical, Standards-Based Exercises for College Students* (Chicago: American Library Association, 2003).

6. Sara Spinks, "Adolescent Brains Are Works in Progress," PBS *Frontline* (31 January 2002). Available at http://www.pbs.org/wgbh/pages/frontline/shows/teenbrain/work/adolescent.html (accessed on 12 July 2005).

7. Ibid.

CHAPTER 8: IT'S NOT MY FAULT: EXCUSES, EXCUSES, EXCUSES

1. Howard Snyder, "Juvenile Arrests 2002," *Office of Juvenile Justice and Delinquency Prevention: Juvenile Justice Bulletin* (September 2002): 1

2. "Fact Sheet," National Campaign to Prevent Teen Pregnancy (Washington, D.C. 2004).

ABOUT THE AUTHOR

Jay Strack, president and founder of Student Leadership University, is an inspiring and effective communicator, author, and minister. Acclaimed by leaders in the business world, religious affiliations, and education realms as a dynamic speaker, Jay has spoken to an estimated 15 million people in his 30 years of ministry. His versatile style has been presented across the country and in 22 countries, before government officials, corporate groups, numerous professional sports teams in the NFL, NBA, and MLB, to over 9,500 school assemblies, and at some 100 universities. Zig Ziglar calls Jay Strack, "entertaining, but powerful, inspiring and informative."

STUDENT LEADERSHIP UNIVERSITY STUDY GUIDES

8 Essentials for a Life of Significance • 1-4185-0598-6

Identity Theft: The Thieves Who Want to Rob Your Future • 1-4185-0594-3

Leadership Rocks: Becoming a Student of Influence • 1-4185-0593-5

Life: How to Get There From Here • 1-4185-0599-4

Mercury Rising: 8 Issues That Are Too Hot to Handle 1-4185-0592-7

Revolution: Effective Campus and Personal Evangelism • 1-4185-0595-1

The Covering: God's Plan to Protect You in the Midst of Spiritual Warfare • 1-4185-0600-1

Worship in the Storm: Navigating Life's Adversities • 1-4185-0597-8

STUDENT LEADERSHIP UNIVERSITY

is committed to providing students with the tools they need to experience Scripture in their daily lives on six levels—see it, hear it, write it, memorize it, pray it, and share it.

Follow SLU and never follow again!